Experimenting with Everyday Science

Sports

Experimenting with Everyday Science

Art and Architecture

Food

Man-Made Materials

Music

Sports

Tools and Machines

Experimenting with Everyday Science

Sports

Stephen M. Tomecek

CHELSEA HOUSE
PUBLISHERS
An imprint of Infobase Publishing

*To my wife Lynn, my favorite athlete, who taught me the
value of staying fit and inspires me to do better every day!*

Experimenting with Everyday Science: Sports

Copyright © 2010 by Infobase Publishing

Chelsea House
An imprint of Infobase Publishing
132 West 31st Street
New York, NY 10001

Library of Congress Cataloging-in-Publication Data

Tomecek, Steve.
  Sports / by Stephen M. Tomecek.
    p. cm. — (Experimenting with everyday science)
  Includes bibliographical references and index.
  ISBN 978-1-60413-170-3 (hardcover)
  1. Sports sciences—Juvenile literature. I. Title. II. Series.
  GV558.T65 2010
  796—dc22   2009022334

Chelsea House books are available at special discounts when purchased in bulk quantities for businesses, associations, institutions, or sales promotions. Please call our Special Sales Department in New York at (212) 967-8800 or (800) 322-8755.

You can find Chelsea House on the World Wide Web at http://www.chelseahouse.com

Text design by Annie O'Donnell
Cover design by Alicia Post
Composition by Mary Susan Ryan-Flynn
Cover printed by Bang Printing, Brainerd, MN
Book printed and bound by Bang Printing, Brainerd, MN
Date printed: May 2010
Printed in the United States of America

10 9 8 7 6 5 4 3 2 1

This book is printed on acid-free paper.

All links and web addresses were checked and verified to be correct at the time of publication. Because of the dynamic nature of the web, some addresses and links may have changed since publication and may no longer be valid.

Contents

Introduction   7

Safety Precautions   8

1 The Scientific Athlete   11

Experiment 1: Feeling Your Pulse   13

Experiment 2: Staying in Balance   18

Experiment 3: Measuring Human Reaction Time   23

Experiment 4: Measuring Body Flexibility   29

Experiment 5: Pushing Muscles to the Limit   34

Experiment 6: Running Distances vs. Speed   39

2 May the Force Be with (or Against) You!   44

Experiment 7: How Gravity Affects Jumping   45

Experiment 8: Controlling How Fast Objects Can Fall   50

Experiment 9: How the Angle at which an
    Object Is Thrown Affects Distance   56

Experiment 10: How Shoe Design Affects Friction   61

Experiment 11: How Lubricant Affects Friction   67

Experiment 12: Testing Your Center of Gravity   73

3 The Spin Is In   77

Experiment 13: How Spinning Wheel Speed Affects Balance   78

Experiment 14: Testing the Speed of Rotation   82

Experiment 15: Throwing a Football   86

Experiment 16: Testing the Spin of a Spherical Ball   90

4 Actions and Reactions   95

Experiment 17: Applying Newton's Laws of Motion   96

Experiment 18: Testing a Ball's Ability to Bounce   101

Experiment 19: Hitting a Ball on a Baseball Bat's "Sweet Spot"   107

Experiment 20: How a Leg Acts Like a Lever   112

Experiment 21: How Resonance Affects Motion   117

5 Smash and Crash   121

Experiment 22: How Mass and Velocity
Affect Momentum of a Moving Object   122

Experiment 23: Changing the Impulse of a Force on a Soccer Ball   127

Experiment 24: The Force of Colliding Objects   132

Experiment 25: Testing Safety Helmet Materials   137

6 Technology and the Future of Sports   141

Glossary   148

Bibliography   150

Further Resources   151

Picture Credits   153

Index   154

About the Author   160

Introduction

When you hear the word *science*, what's the first thing that comes to mind? If you are like most people, it's probably an image of a laboratory filled with tons of glassware and lots of sophisticated equipment. The person doing the science is almost always wearing a white lab coat and probably is looking rather serious while engaged in some type of experiment. While there are many places where this traditional view of a scientist still holds true, labs aren't the only place where science is at work. Science can also be found at construction sites, on a basketball court, and at a concert by your favorite band. The truth of the matter is that science is happening all around us. It's at work in the kitchen when we cook a meal, and we can even use it when we paint a picture. Architects use science when they design a building, and science also explains why your favorite baseball player can hit a home run.

In **Experimenting with Everyday Science**, we are going to examine some of the science that we use in our day-to-day lives. Instead of just talking about the science, these books are designed to put the science right in your hands. Each book contains about 25 experiments centering on one specific theme. Most of the materials used in the experiments are things that you can commonly find around your house or school. Once you are finished experimenting, it is our hope that you will have a better understanding of how the world around you works. While reading these books may not make you a world-class athlete or the next top chef, we hope that they inspire you to discover more about the science behind everyday things and encourage you to make the world a better place!

Safety Precautions

REVIEW BEFORE STARTING ANY EXPERIMENT

Each experiment includes special safety precautions that are relevant to that particular project. These do not include all the basic safety precautions that are necessary whenever you are working on a scientific experiment. For this reason, it is necessary that you read and remain mindful of the General Safety Precautions that follow.

Experimental science can be dangerous, and good laboratory procedure always includes carefully following basic safety rules. Things can happen very quickly while you are performing an experiment. Materials can spill, break, or even catch fire. There will be no time after the fact to protect yourself. Always prepare for unexpected dangers by following the basic safety guidelines during the entire experiment, whether or not something seems dangerous to you at a given moment.

We have been quite sparing in prescribing safety precautions for the individual experiments. For one reason, we want you to take very seriously every safety precaution that is printed in this book. If you see it written here, you can be sure that it is here because it is absolutely critical.

Read the safety precautions here and at the beginning of each experiment before performing each activity. It is difficult to remember a long set of general rules. By rereading these general precautions every time you set up an experiment, you will be reminding yourself that lab safety is critically important. In addition, use your good judgment and pay close attention when performing potentially dangerous procedures. Just because the text does not say "be careful with hot liquids" or "don't cut yourself with a knife" does not mean that you can be careless when boiling water or punching holes in plastic bottles. Notes in the text are special precautions to which you must pay special attention.

GENERAL SAFETY PRECAUTIONS

Accidents caused by carelessness, haste, insufficient knowledge, or taking an unnecessary risk can be avoided by practicing safety procedures and being alert while conducting experiments. Be sure to check the individual experiments in this book for additional safety regulations and adult supervision requirements. If you will be working in a lab, do not work alone. When you are working off site, keep in groups with a minimum of three students per group, and follow school rules and state legal requirements for the number of supervisors required. Ask an adult supervisor with basic training in first aid to carry a small first-aid kit. Make sure everyone knows where this person will be during the experiment.

PREPARING

- Clear all surfaces before beginning experiments.
- Read the instructions before you start.
- Know the hazards of the experiments and anticipate dangers.

PROTECTING YOURSELF

- Follow the directions step-by-step.
- Do only one experiment at a time.
- Locate exits, fire blanket and extinguisher, master gas and electricity shut-offs, eyewash, and first-aid kit.
- Make sure there is adequate ventilation.
- Do not horseplay.
- Keep floor and workspace neat, clean, and dry.
- Clean up spills immediately.
- If glassware breaks, do not clean it up; ask for teacher assistance.
- Tie back long hair.
- Never eat, drink, or smoke in the laboratory or workspace.
- Do not eat or drink any substances tested unless expressly permitted to do so by a knowledgeable adult.

USING EQUIPMENT WITH CARE

- Set up apparatus far from the edge of the desk.
- Use knives or other sharp-pointed instruments with care.
- Pull plugs, not cords, when removing electrical plugs.
- Clean glassware before and after use.
- Check glassware for scratches, cracks, and sharp edges.
- Clean up broken glassware immediately.
- Do not use reflected sunlight to illuminate your microscope.
- Do not touch metal conductors.
- Use alcohol-filled thermometers, not mercury-filled thermometers.

USING CHEMICALS

- Never taste or inhale chemicals.
- Label all bottles and apparatus containing chemicals.
- Read labels carefully.
- Avoid chemical contact with skin and eyes (wear safety glasses, lab apron, and gloves).
- Do not touch chemical solutions.
- Wash hands before and after using solutions.
- Wipe up spills thoroughly.

HEATING SUBSTANCES

- Wear safety glasses, apron, and gloves when boiling water.
- Keep your face away from test tubes and beakers.
- Use test tubes, beakers, and other glassware made of Pyrex glass.
- Never leave apparatus unattended.
- Use safety tongs and heat-resistant gloves.

- If your laboratory does not have heat-proof workbenches, put your Bunsen burner on a heat-proof mat before lighting it.
- Take care when lighting your Bunsen burner; light it with the airhole closed, and use a Bunsen burner lighter in preference to wooden matches.
- Turn off hot plates, Bunsen burners, and gas when you are done.
- Keep flammable substances away from flames and other sources of heat.
- Have a fire extinguisher on hand.

FINISHING UP

- Thoroughly clean your work area and any glassware used.
- Wash your hands.
- Be careful not to return chemicals or contaminated reagents to the wrong containers.
- Do not dispose of materials in the sink unless instructed to do so.
- Clean up all residues and put them in proper containers for disposal.
- Dispose of all chemicals according to all local, state, and federal laws.

BE SAFETY CONSCIOUS AT ALL TIMES!

1

The Scientific Athlete

Do you have a favorite scientist? Is it perhaps Lebron James or Mia Hamm? How about Tony Hawk? If you are confused, you're probably thinking that these people are athletes, not scientists. Even though world-class athletes don't look like Albert Einstein, most understand how gravity, friction, and inertia affect their performance. Whether it's baseball, cycling, gymnastics, or snowboarding, just about any sport you can name has some serious science behind it. An athlete with a working knowledge of the scientific principles at play in a particular sport can have an advantage over competitors.

Most athletes also rely on science to help them prepare to play sports. Science plays a major role in athletic training techniques. It can also help athletes stay healthy. Plus, scientists contribute to the design and manufacture of the latest sports equipment. They work with engineers and other professionals to create everything from low-friction swimsuits to the super-strong, lightweight polymers found in protective padding.

What follows is a look at some of the science behind your favorite sports. It doesn't matter if you're a serious athlete or a fan, understanding the science involved in sports can make the competition that much more enjoyable. Because there are so many sports, it would be impossible to study the science of all of them. Instead, we'll focus on general concepts and principles at work in a variety of sports. Let's begin by looking at some of the science at play in the human body, and some of

There is science at play in every sport, including baseball. Understanding the scientific principles behind a sport can give an athlete—such as Derek Jeter (*batting above*)—an advantage.

the factors that determine whether someone has what it takes to be a superstar.

PHYSICAL FITNESS AND SPORTS

When it comes to sports, **fitness** affects how well an athlete is prepared to play. A fit athlete can handle the **stresses** of competition. Stress comes in different forms. When it comes to sports, people tend to focus on physical stresses. Athletes tend to push their bodies to the limits. They test their strength, speed, endurance, and agility. Smart athletes not only spend time honing their skills, but also work on their physical conditioning.

However, not all stress is physical. Athletes also must deal with the mental stresses brought on by competition and anxiety. Sometimes "butterflies" before a big game can seriously hurt an athlete's ability to perform. In some cases, being a little nervous is a good thing: It can help to get an athlete "pumped up." Finding the proper balance between nervousness and calm is a big part of being mentally fit to play a sport. Training helps an athlete find that balance.

You don't have to be a world-class athlete to worry about being fit. When people engage in physical activity, their bodies change. If our bodies are not prepared for these changes, serious damage and even breakdown may occur. Most of the changes that happen during physical activity are caused by the body's attempt to keep all of our internal systems working at some balanced level. Scientists call this condition **homeostasis**. The term itself comes from two Greek words. *Homeo* means "same" and *stasis* means "standing still." Thus, *homeostasis* means "standing still in the same way" or "staying in balance." To better understand how homeostasis works, we'll begin with a little fitness test. In **Experiment 1:** *Feeling Your Pulse*, you will test to see how your heart rate adjusts when you are physically active.

Feeling Your Pulse

Topic

How does physical activity affect a person's heart rate?

Introduction

The human body is constantly undergoing changes that help to keep it operating under a certain set of "normal" conditions. This process, called homeostasis, is something that happens automatically. We don't have to think about it, and under most conditions, we can't consciously control it. Homeostasis involves a number of body systems working together to control things such as breathing, heart rate, and blood pressure. Homeostasis is especially important for athletes, who often push their bodies to the limit during competition. In this activity, you will test to see how homeostasis works by looking at what happens to your pulse rate when you exercise. Your pulse rate is an indirect measurement of how often your heart beats.

Time Required

45 minutes

Materials

- watch or clock that measures seconds

- chair

- stairs

- two or three friends to serve as additional test subjects

- adult to assist you

Safety Note This experiment depends on changes that occur during moderate exercise and should not pose a risk to a person who is in good health. It is recommended that you conduct this activity under the supervision of a responsible adult. If you have a history of heart or breathing problems, do not do this activity. Please review and follow the safety guidelines.

Procedure

1. Turn your left arm so that your palm is facing up. Extend your arm and put two fingers of your right hand on your left wrist, just below the thumb. This is your pulse point. Figure 1 shows you where to test. You should feel a slight throbbing in your fingers. If you cannot find your pulse on your wrist, try placing two fingers of one hand on your neck, just below your ear.

Pulse point

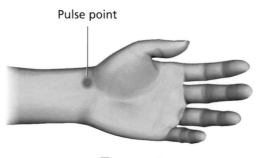

Figure 1

© Infobase Publishing

2. Sit quietly in a chair for one full minute. Then find your pulse in either your wrist or your neck. Have your assistant time you. Count the beats for 15 seconds. Multiply this number by four and record it on the data table next to the heading "Resting Pulse Rate."

3. Walk over to the stairs and step up and down on the first step 30 times. Then immediately take your pulse rate using the technique in Step 2. Record this number on the data table next to the heading "Exercise Pulse Rate."

4. Sit in the chair and wait 30 seconds. Take your pulse rate again and record it on the data table next to the heading "30-second Rest." Continue taking your pulse every minute for the next 5 minutes, recording your pulse on the data table each time.

5. Repeat the experiment with your friends and compare their results with your own.

Data Table 1	
Description	**Pulse Rate (beats per minute)**
Resting Pulse Rate	
Exercise Pulse Rate	
30-second Rest	
90-second Rest	
150-second Rest	
210-second Rest	
270-second Rest	
330-second Rest	

Analysis

1. What happened to your pulse rate when you exercised?
2. Did your pulse rate return to the resting pulse rate as soon as you stopped exercising?
3. What happened to your pulse rate as the time you rested after exercising increased?
4. Why did you have to multiply your pulse rate by four?
5. How did your resting and exercise pulse rate compare to that of your friends?

 What's Going On?

Your pulse gives you an indirect measurement of how fast your heart is beating. When you feel a pulse, you are really sensing the pressure created by your heart as it pumps blood through the arteries of your body. For an average person, a normal resting heart rate is about 72

beats per minute. Marathon runners may have pulse rates in the 40s or 50s. Through exercise and conditioning, they have made their bodies operate more efficiently, so their hearts don't have to work as hard.

The circulation of blood through your body is important. Blood supplies oxygen to your cells, where it is used in a process called respiration. During respiration, cells burn sugar for energy. In the process, they take in oxygen and give off carbon dioxide. When you exercise, the cells of your muscles need more energy, and respiration increases. As a result, muscle cells need more oxygen. Specialized nerve cells measure the amount of oxygen and carbon dioxide in the blood. When the two get out of balance, the nerves send a message to the brain. The brain, in turn, sends a message to the heart and lungs. The heart begins to pump faster and you begin to breathe harder. The result is that the blood delivers more oxygen to the muscle cells. The increase in heart rate continues until you stop exercising. Once you begin to rest, the heart rate begins to slowly return to normal—your resting heart rate. The amount of time it takes for the heart rate to return to the resting heart rate is called the recovery time. In general, the more physically fit you are, the shorter your recovery time will be.

Our Findings

Analysis

1. Exercising increases the pulse rate.
2. The pulse rate after exercising is higher than the resting pulse rate.
3. The longer you rest, the closer the pulse rate gets to the resting pulse rate.
4. Because you are only recording the pulse rate for 15 seconds, multiplying by four gives you a pulse rate number in beats per minute (one minute is 60 seconds).
5. Results will vary from person to person, depending on each person's level of physical fitness.

FEEDBACK SYSTEMS AT WORK AND PLAY

The way our bodies control heart rate is an excellent example of a process that scientists call **feedback**. In a feedback loop, information from some type of sensor is used to make a change in a condition in order to meet some desired goal. All feedback systems have parts that work together to meet a common goal. The first part of the system is a "comparer." Its function is to take information about the current condition from a sensor and compare this information (called input) to some ideal set of conditions. In the case of **Experiment 1:** *Feeling Your Pulse*, the comparer is the brain. It compares information about the oxygen and carbon dioxide levels in the blood to what ideal levels should be. Based on the comparison, the brain then controls one of three "outputs." If the amount of carbon dioxide is too high, the brain sends a message to the heart and lungs via the nervous system to start working faster. If there is too much oxygen compared to carbon dioxide, the brain sends a message to the heart and lungs to slow down. If the oxygen and carbon dioxide levels match the ideal condition, then the brain sends a message that all is well, and the heart and lungs continue at the same rate.

Hundreds of different feedback systems are at work in our bodies. These help to keep us functioning properly at all times. Feedback systems control things like heart rate and blood pressure. They also control the ability to catch a football, shoot a basket, or ski down a mountain slope. In **Experiment 2:** *Staying in Balance*, you will have an opportunity to use feedback as you put your sense of balance to the test.

Staying in Balance

EXPERIMENT 2

Topic

How does the human system of balance work?

Introduction

From surfing and gymnastics to skateboarding and riding a bike, many sports require a good sense of balance. Our ability to balance is controlled by something called the **vestibular system**, which includes our eyes and ears as well as our brains. In this activity, you will test your vestibular system to see how well you can stay in balance under different conditions.

Figure 1

© Infobase Publishing

Time Required

30 minutes

Materials

- 8-ft to 10-ft-long (2.5 m x 3 m) 2 x 4 piece of wood
- 4-ft x 10-ft (1.2 m x 3 m), clear area in a room
- person to assist you

Safety Note It is recommended that you conduct this activity under the supervision of a responsible adult. If you have a problem with balancing or get dizzy easily, do not do this activity. Please review and follow the safety guidelines.

Procedure

1. Make certain that there is no furniture or breakable objects in the clear area. Lay the wood plank on the floor so that the wide side is flat against the floor.

2. Stand at one end of the board. With your hands at your sides, slowly walk next to the board, placing one foot in front of the other until you reach the other end. Then turn around and walk back.

3. Return to the starting point. This time, stand on top of the board. Walk the length of the board with your hands at your sides, placing one foot in front of the other until you reach the other end. Then, without getting off the board, turn around and walk back.

4. Repeat Step 3 with your eyes closed. Have your assistant tell you when you reach the end of the board so you know when to turn around.

5. Repeat Step 4 three more times. Each time, compare your performance with the time before.

6. Return to the starting point. Slowly turn your body in a circle 10 times. Then immediately walk on top of the board with your eyes open as you did in Step 3.

Analysis

1. How did walking on the board with your eyes open compare with walking alongside of the board?

2. How did walking on the board with your eyes closed compare to walking with your eyes open?

3. What happened to your ability to walk on the board with your eyes closed after you repeated the experiment several times?

4. What happened to your ability to walk on the board after you spun around?

What's Going On?

The human vestibular system allows us to maintain our sense of balance, or equilibrium. Several sense organs play a role in balancing. These include our eyes and ears, as well as specialized, pressure-sensing cells in our arms and legs. As you probably discovered in this experiment, trying to walk and balance with your eyes closed is more difficult than walking with your eyes open. That's because the eyes provide the brain with information about where to put the feet. If you continue to walk with your eyes closed, however, it becomes easier. Your brain has stored some of the information that it needs for you to complete the task. Also, instead of getting input from the eyes, your brain begins relying more on input from your arms and legs. Through practice, you condition your brain to bypass input from your eyes.

The eyes are important for us in maintaining our balance, but the ears perform a much larger role. Our ears are divided into three parts. The innermost part of the ear is known as the labyrinth. The organs that control balance are here. Inside the labyrinth are three fluid-filled tubes set at right angles to one another. These are called the semicircular canals. At the end of each of each

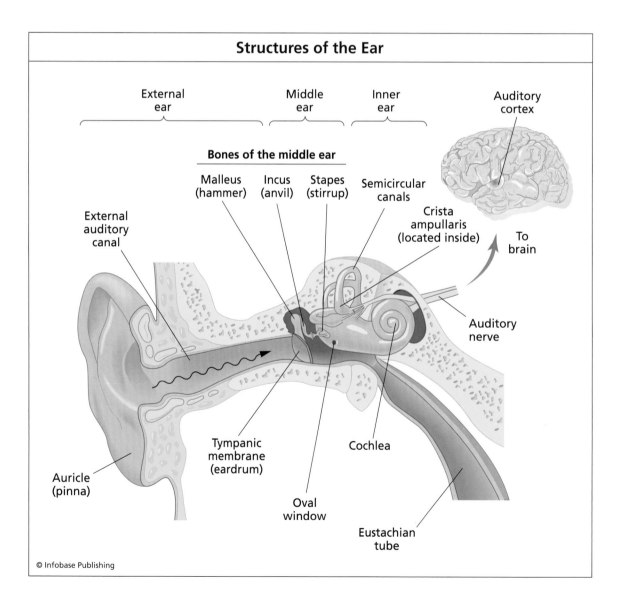

Structures of the Ear

External ear

Middle ear

Inner ear

Auditory cortex

Bones of the middle ear

Malleus (hammer)

Incus (anvil)

Stapes (stirrup)

Semicircular canals

Crista ampullaris (located inside)

To brain

External auditory canal

Auditory nerve

Tympanic membrane (eardrum)

Cochlea

Auricle (pinna)

Oval window

Eustachian tube

canal is an organ called the crista. The crista contains a mass of tiny hairs that are connected to the brain via nerves. The fluid in the semicircular canal presses against the outer part of the crista. When we move our heads from side to side, the fluid moves back and forth, changing the pressure on the crista. This signals to the brain that our body position has changed. In turn, the brain sends signals to our arms and legs to reposition our bodies, allowing us to balance.

If a person spins in a circle or turns upside down, the fluid in the semicircular canals "sloshes" around. As a result, the brain is flooded with conflicting signals about the body's position. This makes it difficult to balance. After a time, the fluid settles down, and the brain starts to receive normal signals again. Only then can we regain our ability to balance. This can be a problem for gymnasts or skaters who spin and turn frequently. They can condition their brains to overcome the sensory disruption, but it takes a great deal of work.

Our Findings

1. Walking on the floor next to the board is generally easier than walking on top of the board.
2. Walking with your eyes closed is more difficult than with your eyes open.
3. The more attempts you make with your eyes closed, the better you can balance on the board.
4. It is more difficult to balance on the board after spinning around.

SPEED VS. QUICKNESS

One of the most important qualities of an athlete is speed. When scientists talk about speed, they are usually referring to the amount of time it takes for an athlete to get from one place to another. Whether it's a sprinter running a race or a NASCAR driver in the Daytona 500, speed is measured in terms of some unit of distance divided by some unit of time. Typical speeds are measured in meters per second or miles per hour. In sports such as track, swimming, and drag racing, speed determines the winner. Yet, speed is not the same as quickness. When scientists talk about the quickness of an athlete, they are interested in **reaction time**. This is the measurement of how long it takes for a living thing to react to some type of change, and it's another example of feedback in action. In **Experiment 3:** *Measuring Human Reaction Time*, you and a friend will test each other's reaction times to discover just how quick you are.

EXPERIMENT 3

Measuring Human Reaction Time

Topic

How can human reaction time be measured? Does it change over time?

Introduction

An individual's reaction time is a measure of how fast the person responds to some type of external stimulus. It is different from speed, which is a measure of how much time it takes for something to move a given distance. A fast reaction time helps people to avoid problems or situations that may cause harm. For example, when driving, a quick reaction time can mean the difference between a deadly accident and a near miss. Reaction time also is critical in many sports. A soccer goalie must react quickly to block a shot, and a baseball player must react quickly to hit a fastball. In this activity, you and a partner will take turns measuring each other's reaction times.

Time Required

45 minutes

Materials

- 12-in.-long (30-cm) wooden or plastic ruler

- person to assist you

Safety Note   No special safety precautions are needed for this activity. Please review and follow the safety guidelines before proceeding.

Procedure

1. Stand facing your partner. Hold the ruler between your thumb and forefinger near the 12 in. (30 cm) end. Have your partner hold his or her open

hand directly below the other end of the ruler. Your partner's hand should be open enough so that the ruler can fall between his or her thumb and forefinger. No part of your partner's hand should touch the ruler. The setup should look like Figure 1.

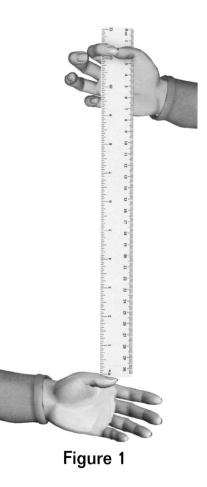

Figure 1

2. As soon as you let go of the ruler, your partner will have to catch it by closing his or her hand. Without warning, let go of the ruler. Use the markings on the ruler to measure how far the ruler dropped. Measure at the point where your partner's thumb rests on the ruler, and record that number on the data table under "Trial 1." If your partner misses the ruler entirely, record the word *miss*.

3. Repeat the experiment nine more times, and record the catch point on the ruler on the data sheet each time.

4. Reverse the roles so that your partner drops the ruler and you try to catch it. Record the catch points on the data sheet for each trial.

Data Table 1		
Trials	**Your Partner's Catches**	**Your Catches**
Trial 1		
Trial 2		
Trail 3		
Trial 4		
Trial 5		
Trial 6		
Trial 7		
Trial 8		
Trial 9		
Trial 10		

Analysis

1. What was the only clue that your partner had that you were dropping the ruler?
2. How do different catch points on the ruler relate to the reaction time of the person who is catching it?
3. In general, what happened to the reaction times of the person catching the ruler as the number of trials increased?

What's Going On?

Reaction time is an example of a feedback system at work in our bodies. Feedback involves the brain getting information from a sense organ and then using that information to make some type of change. In this particular experiment, the feedback happens when the eyes of the person trying to catch the ruler send a message to the brain that the ruler has begun to fall. The brain then sends a message to the person's hand to grab the ruler. The time between the person seeing the ruler fall and moving to catch it is the reaction time. Reaction times vary from one person to the next, but scientists have found that the average person has a reaction time of about 0.20 seconds, or twenty-hundredths of a second. World-class athletes are usually much quicker and often have reaction times as short as 0.13 seconds (thirteen-hundredths of a second). That may not sound like a big difference, but it can be the difference between blocking a shot and giving up the winning goal.

In this activity, you can use the falling ruler to indirectly measure reaction time. Because the ruler is falling due to the force of gravity, and because the acceleration of a falling body due to gravity is a known rate, the distance the ruler falls equals a predictable amount of time. If you catch the ruler at the 6-in. or 15-cm mark, the ruler has fallen 6 in. or 15 cm. This translates to a reaction time of about 0.18 seconds. If the ruler falls 8 in. or 20 cm, the reaction time is about 0.20 seconds. The chart below shows the reaction time for different fall distances. If you find the distances on your data sheet on the first column of the chart, you can get an approximate value for your reaction time.

Distance Ruler Falls	Reaction Time in Seconds
5 in. or 12 cm	0.16
6 in. or 15 cm	0.18
7 in. or 17 cm	0.19
8 in. or 20 cm	0.20
9 in. or 22 cm	0.22
10 in. or 25 cm	0.23

Reaction time is not always the same for most people. When you are tired, you tend to react slower. When you are excited, you tend to react faster. After a few trials of the ruler drop experiment, reaction time usually gets faster. Then, after a few more trials, it normally slows down. This is because at first, a person is consciously trying to react quickly. His or her senses are heightened. But a person's body can't maintain this focus for long. Fatigue starts to set in. As a person gets tired, reaction time starts to slow.

Our Findings

1. The cue is seeing the ruler start to fall.
2. The higher the number on the ruler, the longer the reaction time.
3. Results will vary, but a typical data set will have reaction time increasing at first and then decreasing.

ELEMENTS OF PHYSICAL CONDITIONING

High-level athletes spend a great deal of time training. Even the most gifted athlete has to stay in good physical shape. Working out on a regular basis helps athletes maintain peak performance levels and reduces the amount of time they need to recover from the stress of competition.

Even for the nonathlete, physical conditioning is important. Being physically fit allows people to get through a day without becoming exhausted. Proper conditioning also gives people an **energy** reserve to meet unexpected challenges, such as running after a missed school bus or chasing after a runaway pet. In **Experiment 1:** *Feeling Your Pulse*, you discovered the connection between heart rate and physical activity. In the next three activities, you will test your own level of performance in three other measures of fitness. We'll begin with **Experiment 4:** *Measuring Body Flexibility*, where you will measure your body's flexibility and discover how being mobile is a key part of every sport.

A great athlete must be physically fit. Here, Serbian tennis player Jelena Jankovic stretches to hit a return ball in a match against Venus Williams during the 2007 U.S. Open.

Measuring Body Flexibility

Topic

How can you measure your body's flexibility?

Introduction

Having a high degree of body flexibility is important not only for athletes, but also for the average person who must manage the rigors of daily life. A person is flexible when he or she has a full range of motion at every joint in the body. Joints are places where two bones connect or join together. If a person is not flexible, it will be difficult to run, bend, lift, or reach in different directions. Being flexible is especially important for athletes. It makes them less likely to get hurt from falls and reduces the chances of muscle strains and tears. In this activity, you will test your general level of flexibility by conducting a full-body stretch. Read the safety notes before doing the activity.

Time Required

30 minutes

Materials

- yardstick or meterstick

- roll of masking tape

- person to assist you

Safety Note   It is recommended that you conduct this activity under the supervision of a responsible adult. Before doing the test, stretch a few times by <u>slowly</u> bending over and touching your knees. When doing the test, avoid jerking or bouncing motions. Bend slowly with a gradual motion.

Procedure

1. Clear an open area on the floor large enough for you to lie flat on your back. Tear off a piece of masking tape about 6 in. or 15 cm long and place it on the floor near one end of the space.

2. Lay the yardstick flat on the floor so that it crosses the piece of masking tape. The 36 in. or 100 cm end should be pointed away from the clear space. The stick should cross the tape exactly at the 15 in. or 38 cm mark. Place one piece of masking tape across each end of the ruler, taping it to the floor.

3. Take off your shoes and socks, and sit on the floor with your legs outstretched so that your heels are just touching the tape. The 1 in. or 1 cm end of the ruler should be between your legs, and your heels should be right on the tape so that they rest at the 15 in. or 38 cm mark of the ruler. Your feet should be about 6 in. or 15 cm apart. The whole setup should look like Figure 1.

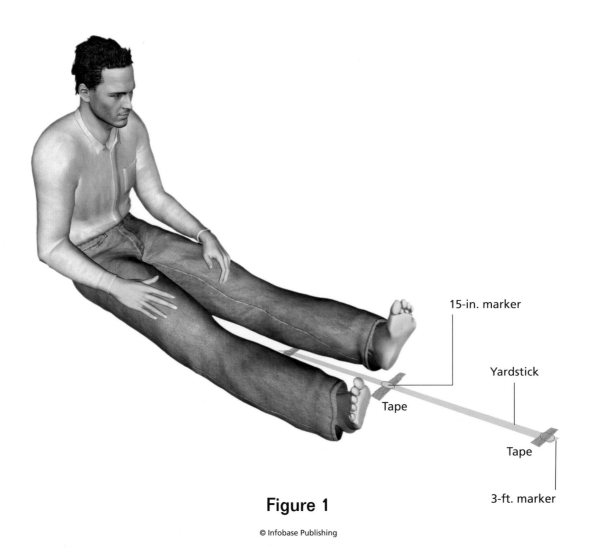

15-in. marker

Yardstick

Tape

Tape

3-ft. marker

Figure 1

4. Slowly bend forward, reaching with both hands outstretched and overlapping each other. Your hands should be directly over the ruler. Lean as far forward as possible. (If you feel any pain, stop immediately.) When you reach your maximum stretch, record the number that your fingertips reach on the yardstick. Lie back down flat on the floor and rest for 10 seconds.

5. Repeat Step 4 three more times, each time measuring and recording the maximum stretch distance on the data table.

Data Table 1	
Trial Number	**Maximum Stretch**
1	
2	
3	
4	

Analysis

1. Why is it important to warm up before doing the stretch test?
2. What happened to the maximum stretch distance as the number of trials increased?
3. Why is it important not to jerk or bounce when you do the test?
4. What limitations does this test have when it comes to measuring total body flexibility?

What's Going On?

At joints, bones are connected by sets of muscles. In order to make the bones at a joint move, the muscles alternately contract (get shorter) and relax (get longer). Over time, when people play sports, exercise, or simply move around doing daily routines, the muscles—as well as the ligaments that connect muscles to the bones—usually get shorter and tighter. This reduces the range of motion at the joints, making our bodies feel stiff and less flexible. The stretch test does not tell you the flexibility of all your muscles, but it does give you a general sense of flexibility because it requires that you use most of the muscles in your arms, legs, back, and neck. Results vary by age, weight, and gender. If you were able to reach between 13 in. and 19 in. (33 cm and 48 cm), your flexibility is about average. If you were able to reach beyond the 20 in. (50 cm) mark, you have good flexibility. If you reached only the 8 in. (20 cm) mark or less, you probably need to work on increasing your body flexibility.

When you did the stretch test, you may have noticed that you could stretch a little farther each time. Each time you stretch a muscle, special receptors called "muscle spindles" send messages to your spinal cord, alerting it to the fact that the muscle is being lengthened. When muscles are slowly stretched, they become more elastic. This allows them to get a little longer each time they are used. If you try to quickly stretch a muscle, your body reacts with something called the stretch reflex. In this case, the spinal cord protects the muscle by sending a message telling it to contract. If you try to force a muscle to stretch while it is contracting, you run the risk of a tear in either the muscle itself or the ligaments that hold it to a bone.

The best way to maintain body flexibility is to do periodic stretching exercises. If you have watched athletes before they compete, they almost always warm up by doing a series of stretches. Even for nonathletes, regular stretching is important. It improves body posture and reduces muscle soreness. Practicing yoga and t'ai chi are two good ways to keep flexible.

Our Findings

1. Warming up before doing physical exercise helps to prestretch muscles, which reduces the chances that they will get strained.
2. Answers will vary by person, but in general, the stretch distance will increase as you conduct more trials.
3. Sudden movements, such as jerking or bouncing, can strain or tear muscle fibers.
4. The full-body stretch tests the flexibility of many body joints but does not cover every one.

MAKING MUSCLES

Bodies move because of the interactions of muscles and bones. The bones of the skeleton form the framework of the human body, but muscles make the bones move. As we saw in the previous experiment, movement of the skeleton is possible because of the different joints that connect our bones. At most joints, there are two muscles that work together. These muscles are usually found on opposite sides of the bone. When one contracts, the other relaxes.

To understand this motion better, let's take a close-up look at what happens when you bend your arm at the elbow: Take your right arm and stretch it straight out in front of you with your palm facing up. Place your left hand under your right elbow, and slowly bend your forearm so that your right hand comes toward your head. As your forearm moves, you should feel the bones of your arm pivot at the elbow. Hold your arm straight out again; this time, rest your left hand on top of your right arm, between your elbow and shoulder. Slowly bend your arm again. This time you should feel the top of your arm bulge a bit. This bulge is coming from your biceps muscle. To make your arm bend, your biceps contracts, or gets shorter. As it does, the muscle fibers bunch together, causing a bulge in your arm.

Hold your right arm straight out again. Place your left hand beneath your arm, between the elbow and your armpit. You should feel a small bulge under the skin. This is your triceps muscle. Bend your arm again; the bulge gets smaller. As you bend your arm, the triceps muscle relaxes, causing the muscle fibers to stretch.

Athletes work out to condition and build muscle strength, but they also build **muscle endurance**, too. This is a measure of how long or how often a set of muscles can be used before the muscles need to rest. In **Experiment 5:** *Pushing Muscles to the Limit*, you will put your own muscles to the test by seeing how long you can conduct a simple exercise.

Pushing Muscles to the Limit

Topic

How do muscles behave when they are used for an extended period of time?

Introduction

Our bodies need a constant supply of energy to function properly. Most of this energy comes from the food we eat, which is broken down by the process of digestion into a simple sugar called glucose. Glucose is also known as blood sugar, and, as that name suggests, it is carried by the blood to individual cells. There, it reacts with oxygen in a process called oxidation to form a chemical called **adenosine triphosphate** (**ATP**). Under low-stress conditions, oxidation of glucose can form enough ATP to keep a body going. During exercise, muscle cells need more energy than oxidation can deliver. In this activity, you will experience what happens to the muscles of your arms when the normal oxidation of glucose isn't enough.

Time Required

30 minutes

Materials

- clear space on the floor next to a wall
- person to assist you
- stopwatch or timing device that measures seconds

Safety Note This experiment depends on changes that occur during moderate exercise and should not pose a risk to a person who is in good health. It is recommended that you conduct this activity under the supervision of a responsible adult. If you have a history of heart or breathing problems, do not do this activity. Please review and follow the safety guidelines.

Procedure

1. Clear an area on the floor next to a wall. Lie flat on the floor on your stomach, with your feet touching the wall and your hands underneath your body in a pre-push-up position, as shown in Figure 1.

Figure 1

© Infobase Publishing

2. Have your assistant prepare to time you as you do a push-up. When your assistant says "go," extend your arms and push up. Hold your body off the floor in this elevated position as long as you can. Have your assistant time how many seconds you stay that way, and record the number on the data table next to the heading "Trial 1."

3. After doing the first trial, rest on the floor for 30 seconds. Repeat step 2. Have your assistant record the number of seconds you stay elevated this time next to the heading "Trial 2." Repeat the test one more time, recording the result next to the heading "Trial 3."

4. After completing Trial 3, rest for a full 10 minutes. Then repeat step 2. Record the results on the data sheet next to the heading "Trial 4."

Data Table 1	
Trials	**Seconds**
Trial 1	
Trial 2	
Trial 3	
Trial 4	

Analysis

1. How did the muscles of your arms feel after completing the first trial?
2. What happened to the time you were able to keep your body elevated as you went from Trial 1 to Trial 3?
3. How did the muscles of your arms feel during Trial 3?
4. How did your time in Trial 4 compare to your times for the first three trials?

 ## What's Going On?

When it comes to playing sports or doing exercise, one of the biggest problems that athletes face is muscle fatigue. That's the ache that happens when muscles become overloaded. In this activity, you got to experience muscle fatigue firsthand. When you do strenuous exercise, your muscle cells require more ATP to keep them energized. At first, the rate of oxidation increases. As a result, the heart pumps faster, and you begin to breathe harder. As long as there is enough oxygen to meet the energy needs of the muscle cells, ATP can form from the oxidation of glucose. Sometimes, muscle activity becomes too strenuous, or muscles are made to work for a long time. Then, the normal **aerobic** process of oxidation (*aerobic* means "with oxygen") cannot provide enough energy for the muscles. When this happens, muscle cells start to break down fuel molecules without using oxygen. This **anaerobic** ("without oxygen") process is called lactic acid fermentation.

When it comes to fueling muscles, lactic acid fermentation has a serious drawback. In addition to producing ATP, it also makes lactic acid, or lactate which begins to build up in the muscle cells. This is what causes muscle fatigue. When lactate builds up in the muscles, it also makes your blood more acidic. This increases the rate of oxidation even more. Your heart beats faster and you breathe harder. Eventually, your body can't keep up, and you develop what's called an oxygen debt. Your muscles begin to shut down until your body can take in enough oxygen to clear out the lactate. Only then can your muscles begin working normally again.

Our Findings

1. After the first trial, the muscles feel tired, but there should be no pain.
2. In general, as you go from Trial 1 to Trial 3, you cannot hold your body up as long.
3. During Trial 3, you may feel cramping in the muscles of your arms.
4. In Trial 4, you should have been able to hold up your body for a longer time than in Trial 3.

ADVANTAGES OF WEIGHT TRAINING

Some people think of "weight training" and have visions of bodybuilders pumping iron in a gym. Weight training isn't just for weight lifters, though. Athletes in track, swimming, football, baseball, and even tennis all use weight training. It is anaerobic exercise because it does not generally increase the body's use of oxygen. Weight training does increase muscle strength, flexibility, and endurance. To understand how this works, we must take a look at how skeletal muscle is put together.

Skeletal muscle is made of thousands of muscle cells that look like long, threadlike fibers. When you exercise a muscle, the repeated contractions make these fibers thicker. Over time, this not only makes the muscle look bigger, but makes it more efficient. This means that the muscle can carry a heavier load and work for a longer time before fatigue begins.

Weight training involves specific exercises that isolate different muscle groups. A person builds muscle mass by gradually increasing the weight and the number of times each exercise is done, called repetitions or "reps." Over time, the exercised muscle groups become more defined. Bodybuilders take this process to the extreme. This is why they have tremendous muscle definition. Weight training is useful for many athletes, though they may not be looking for large muscles. It makes muscles stronger and quicker to react, giving athletes a competitive edge. Weight training might make the difference for a football running back who has to push through a pile of defenders to get over the goal line, or for a swimmer who has to give that extra kick to hold off an opponent near the finish line.

Runners may use weight training to help build strength in their leg muscles. Not all runners have the same goal, so the type of exercises that each runner does will vary. Sprinters and distance runners will often do different types of weight training. This is because running for distance and running for speed affect muscles differently. In **Experiment 6:** *Running Distances vs. Speed*, you will test to see how your own performance differs depending on the type of race you are running.

EXPERIMENT 6
Running Distances vs. Speed

Topic

How does the distance a runner travels affect the speed of travel?

Introduction

If you have ever watched track events, you've probably noticed that sprinters have a different running style than distance runners do. When you run a race, your body goes through many changes in order to keep your muscles working. World-class runners can maximize their performance by understanding how these changes happen and work with their bodies. In this activity, you will test to see how the distance that you run in a race affects the way that your body performs.

Time Required

45 minutes

Materials

- stopwatch that measures tenths of seconds
- 75-ft-long (25-m) tape measure or a piece of rope cut to 75 ft (25 m) long
- football or soccer field
- 2 cones or similar objects for marking distances
- adult to assist you

Safety Note   This experiment depends on changes that occur during moderate exercise and should not pose a risk to a person who is in good health. It is recommended that you conduct this activity under the supervision of a responsible adult. If you have a history of heart or breathing problems, do not do this activity. Please review and follow the safety guidelines.

Procedure

1. Use the rope or tape measure to mark off a section of the field that is 75 ft (25 m) long. Figure 1 shows how to do this. Use the two cones to set a starting point and an ending point.

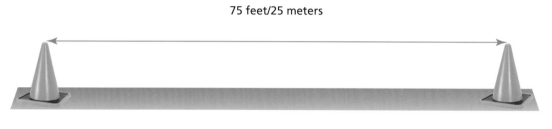

75 feet/25 meters

Figure 1

© Infobase Publishing

2. Do a few stretching exercises to warm up your leg muscles. Go to the starting point. Have the person who is assisting you take the stopwatch and stand at the finish point. When the person who is timing you says "go," run as hard as you can to the finish point. Record your time to the nearest tenth of a second on the data sheet, next to the heading "Trial 1."

3. Rest for 10 minutes. Mark off 300 ft (100 m) on the field and reset the cones at the new distance. Repeat Step 2, and record your time on the data sheet, next to the heading "Trial 2."

4. Rest for 10 minutes. Mark off 450 ft (150 m) on the field, and reset the cones at the new distance. Repeat step 2, and record your time on the data sheet, next to the heading "Trial 3."

5. After recording your last trial, recalculate the times for Trial 2 and Trial 3 to adjust for the increased distance you traveled. Divide your Trial 2 time by four, and your Trial 3 time by six. Record these times on the data sheet under the heading "Adjusted Time."

6. Repeat the experiment with your friends, and compare their results with your own.

Data Table 1		
Trials	**Actual Time**	**Adjusted Time**
Trial 1		
Trial 2		Time divided by 4: _____
Trial 3		Time divided by 6: _____

Analysis

1. How did your actual time in Trial 1 compare with your adjusted times in Trial 2 and Trial 3?
2. How did you body feel after running the shortest distance?
3. How did your body feel after running the longest distance?
4. Based on your experiment, why is it important for marathon and other distance runners to pace themselves during a race?

 ## What's Going On?

When you run at full speed, your leg muscles require a great deal of energy. This energy comes from a chemical manufactured in the muscle cells called adenosine triphosphate (ATP). ATP can be created in two ways. Under low-stress conditions, your muscles create ATP using oxygen carried by the blood. Under high-stress conditions, the muscles can also form ATP anaerobically, or without oxygen.

Skeletal muscle is made of two different types of fibers. Type I fibers are also called "slow twitch" muscle fibers. They tend to contract slowly and fire for a longer period of time before they get tired. Type I muscle fibers almost always use oxygen to generate ATP. Type II muscle fibers are known as "fast twitch" muscles. They are designed to contract rapidly. They can supply a sudden burst of energy, but it cannot be sustained for a long time. Type II muscle fibers usually make ATP anaerobically.

If you are running a sprint, your legs will rely on Type II muscles first. Because the race is short, your body usually can produce enough energy by anaerobic respiration. As a result, your time will be fast. Anaerobic respiration creates a waste product called lactic acid, which quickly builds up in muscle cells. After the race, you continue to breathe hard for a few minutes because your body must supply oxygen to the muscle cells to clear out the lactic acid.

When you run longer distances, your body cannot sustain the same pace as it does for a sprint. That's because as the lactic acid builds up in the muscles, it creates an oxygen debt. Eventually, the muscles shut down until the lactic acid can be cleared out. If you compare your adjusted times for the second and third trials, you will see that the longer you run, the slower your times will be. In order to minimize the production of lactic acid in the muscles, distance runners rely on slow-twitch muscle fibers. They pace themselves, keeping their fast-twitch muscles in reserve until they near the finish line. Then they call on these muscle fibers and their anaerobic respiration to provide a sudden "kick" at the end of the race.

Our Findings

Analysis

1. Times will vary, but in general, the time for Trial 1 is faster than the adjusted times for Trial 2 and Trial 3.

2. Depending on your physical condition, you should be slightly out of breath.

3. You should be winded, and you may even experience some cramping in your legs.

4. It is impossible to run at top speed for a long distance because your body cannot keep up the pace for an extended period of time.

THE GENDER GAP

Have you ever wondered why in swimming and track events the top male finishers almost always have faster times than the top female ones? The answer has nothing to do with training techniques, desire, or talent level. Males and females are not put together the same way. Apart from the obvious external differences, men have one major internal difference that gives them a serious advantage over women when it comes to sports that depend on strength and speed. They have more **testosterone**.

Testosterone is a hormone found in both men and women, but the levels in men are much higher. When a boy reaches puberty, the testes start producing large amounts of testosterone. This natural chemical causes men to grow facial hair and allows for larger muscles with more Type II (fast-twitch) muscle fibers. This is one reason why men have the natural ability to lift more weight than women do. Testosterone also allows men to have less natural body fat than women, which is partly why men are faster runners and swimmers. Plus, testosterone increases the amount of hemoglobin in the blood. Hemoglobin is the molecule that transports oxygen to cells. By getting more oxygen from the blood, men's muscles can work longer before fatigue begins.

Having more testosterone does not guarantee that a man will win every competition against a woman. Through training, female athletes can close the gender gap considerably—and many top female athletes are much stronger and faster than the average man. When it comes to world-class athletes setting records, however, men will always be just a little bit faster and stronger, thanks to the advantage that testosterone gives them.

2

May the Force Be with (or Against) You!

When it comes to playing sports, an athlete's ability to understand and control the forces involved in a game goes a long way in determining who wins and loses. **Force** might make people think of the magical powers of the Jedi Knights in the *Star Wars* films. Both Yoda and Luke Skywalker used "the force," but the forces involved in sports are nowhere near as mystical. To a scientist, the word *force* is used to describe natural influences that affect objects. Some typical forces include magnetism, static electricity, and friction.

One important force that athletes must deal with is **gravity**. Gravity is a force of attraction between any objects that have mass. It holds Earth in orbit around the sun, and it also keeps us from flying off the surface of the planet. The effect of gravity comes into play in almost every sport. Gravity works against a high-jumper or basketball player who is trying to "hang" in the air. Yet, without gravity, sports such as skydiving or snowboarding would not be possible.

In many sports, jumping ability plays a critical role in the outcome of a game. In baseball, for example, a high-leaping outfielder might pull a home run back into the park and save the game. In football, a receiver who can jump higher than a defender can catch a winning touchdown. In soccer, a high-flying goalie can make a game-winning save. In **Experiment 7:** *How Gravity Affects Jumping*, you will test to see how good you are at defeating the force of gravity as you put your jumping ability to the test.

EXPERIMENT 7

How Gravity Affects Jumping

Topic

How does gravity affect our ability to jump?

Introduction

Whether it's going up high to receive an "alley-oop" pass, grabbing a rebound, or making a monster slam dunk, some basketball players seem to defy gravity and hang in the air. In fact, announcers often will speak about "hang time" when they discuss a player's ability to jump. In this activity, you will test your own "hang time" and see how you can enhance it.

Time Required

45 minutes

Materials

● high wall

● piece of chalk

● damp paper towel or sponge

● tape measure, yardstick, or meterstick

● stepladder

Safety Note This experiment requires that you do moderate exercise and should not pose a risk to a person who is in good health. It is recommended that you conduct this activity under the supervision of a responsible adult. If you have a history of leg or balance problems, do not do this activity. Please review and follow the safety guidelines.

Procedure

1. Move any furniture or objects away from the wall so that you have a clear space for about 9 ft (3 m) out from the wall. The ceiling should be high enough so that you cannot reach it by jumping up.

2. Stand flat-footed, facing the wall. With a piece of chalk in your hand, stretch your arm up as high as you can, and make a small mark on the wall. Use the tape measure to measure the height of the mark from the floor to the nearest centimeter or inch, and record it on the data sheet under each of the headings labeled "Starting Height."

3. Do a few deep knee bends to warm up your leg muscles. Take a practice jump. Jump straight up, parallel to the wall from a flat-footed stance. Do not take any steps before jumping, and do not jump into the wall.

Figure 1

© Infobase Publishing

4. After taking your practice jump, jump three more times. Use the chalk to mark the highest point that you reach on the wall each time you jump. Use the ladder and tape measure to measure the height of each chalk mark, and record it on the data table below under the trials for the heading "Standing Jump." When you have finished recording the data, use the damp towel to erase the chalk marks.

5. On the data sheet, subtract the starting height value from the trial height value for each of the three standing jumps, and record it on the line labeled "Jump Height." Add the jump heights and divide by three. This will give you the average height of your standing vertical jump.

6. Next, you are going to test your jumping ability after a short run. Move to one end of the clear area and take a practice jump. Start with your feet together and take three large steps parallel to the wall before jumping. Do not run toward the wall.

7. After taking your practice jump, jump three more times. Hold the chalk in the hand that is closest to the wall. When you reach the highest point of your jump, make a mark on the wall. After you have finished each jump, use the ladder to measure the height of the chalk mark, and record it on the data table next to the trials for the heading "Running Jump." When you have finished recording the data, use the damp towel to erase the chalk marks.

8. On the data table, subtract the starting height value from the trial height value for each of the three running jumps, and record it on the line labeled "Jump Height." Add the jump heights together and divide by three. This will give you the average height of your running vertical jump.

Data Table 1
Standing Jump
Trial 1 _____ – Starting Height _____ = Jump Height ____
Trial 2 _____ – Starting Height _____ = Jump Height ____
Trial 3 _____ – Starting Height _____ = Jump Height ____
Total Jump Height _____ / 3 = Average Jump Height _____
Running Jump
Trial 1 _____ – Starting Height _____ = Jump Height ____
Trial 2 _____ – Starting Height _____ = Jump Height ____
Trial 3 _____ – Starting Height _____ = Jump Height ____
Total Jump Height _____ / 3 = Average Jump Height _____

Analysis

1. How did the height of your average standing jump compare to your average running jump?

2. What caused the difference between standing and running?

3. Why did you conduct three trials for each type of jump and use the average instead of just doing one jump for each?

 ## What's Going On?

When you jump up, gravity pulls your body back down. As soon as your feet leave the ground, the force of gravity begins to slow you down until your body stops gaining height. At this point, you reverse direction and begin to fall. When you jump, the force that propels you up comes from your leg muscles and your feet pushing against the ground. The greater the pushing force, the higher your speed will be when you leave the ground and the higher you will jump. The higher you jump, the longer you will hang in the air. When you try to jump straight up from a flat-footed stance, your leg muscles cannot generate much vertical speed. When you take several steps before jumping, your body is already in motion. When you jump, this motion is added to the jump, giving you more speed, which allows you to jump higher and hang longer in the air. When basketball players go up for a slam dunk, they usually take a running start. Only players with exceptional jumping ability (or those who are extremely tall) can dunk a ball standing flat-footed. It may seem as if some players can hang in the air for long periods of time, but even the best basketball players have a hang time of only about one second.

Our Findings

1. While the numbers will vary, the running jump height should have been greater than the standing jump height.

2. When you take a few steps before jumping, you are traveling up at a greater velocity than when you are standing flat-footed on the ground.

3. Doing three trials for each jump gives you more consistent results and minimizes the effects of a single bad jump.

FALLING BODIES

As you discovered in the previous experiment, no matter how high you jump, you will eventually be pulled back to the surface of Earth by the force of gravity. Gravity doesn't just affect things that are moving up. If you hold a ball in your outstretched hand and let it go, the force of gravity will cause it to fall back to the ground. When you first let go of the ball, it will fall slowly. Yet, the farther it drops, the faster it will fall.

When a moving object gains or loses speed, scientists say that it is undergoing **acceleration**. Back in the 1500s, Galileo determined that gravity causes falling objects to accelerate at a regular, predictable rate.

On Earth, the acceleration due to gravity is a constant, usually represented by the symbol g. It has a value of 32 feet/sec^2 (9.8 meters per sec^2). An object that falls increases its speed by 9.8 meters per second for each second that it falls. In other words, if you drop a ball and it falls for one second, it will have a speed of 9.8 meters per second when it hits the ground. If you drop the same ball for a greater height and it falls for two seconds, it will be traveling at twice the speed, or 64 feet/sec^2 (19.6 meters per sec), when it hits the ground. There is another factor that affects how fast an object will fall. In **Experiment 8: *Controlling How Fast Objects Can Fall***, you will test and see how balls of different sizes, masses, and shapes react when they are dropped from the same height.

Controlling How Fast Objects Can Fall

Topic

What factors control how fast an object will fall?

Introduction

Estimating how fast an object will be moving when it hits the ground (or a player's outstretched hand) is a critical part of many sports. Back in the late 1500s, Galileo Galilei discovered that the speed at which an object falls is controlled by the force of gravity. At this time, most people believed that the heavier an object was, the faster it would fall. In conducting his experiments, Galileo discovered that this was not always the case. He also found that the speed of a falling body could be affected by forces other than gravity. In this activity, you will test to see how the mass, size, and shape of a ball affect its speed and determine what forces play a role in how fast it falls.

Time Required

45 minutes

Materials

- baseball
- tennis ball
- ping-pong ball
- golf ball
- 2 footballs that are the same size and weight
- partner to assist you
- sturdy chair or stepladder

Procedure

1. Place the chair or ladder in a clear space in the middle of a room. Have your partner hold the chair or ladder. Carefully stand on top of the chair. If you are using a ladder, stand no higher than the second step.

2. Hold the golf ball in one hand and the tennis ball in the other. Compare the weight of the two balls. They should be almost the same. Predict which will hit the ground first when you drop them from the same height. Stretch your hands in front of you and hold the balls so their bottoms are the same height from the ground (see Figure 1.) Let them go at the same time, and have your partner observe which hits the ground first. Repeat

Figure 1

© Infobase Publishing

the experiment two more times, and record your observations on the data table.

3. Repeat Step 2, using the baseball and the tennis ball. In this test, the two balls are about the same size, but the baseball has more mass. Predict which will hit the ground first. Drop them from the same height and repeat the experiment three times. Record your observations on the data table.

4. Repeat Step 2 again, but use the golf ball and the ping-pong ball. These two balls also are the same size, but the masses are different. Repeat the experiment three times, and record your observations on the data table.

5. Repeat Step 2 again. This time use the two footballs. It is important that the two balls have the same size and mass. Hold one ball so that the pointed ends are facing up and down (vertically). Hold the other ball so that the ends are sideways. Make certain that the point of the first ball is exactly even with the bottom of the second ball. Predict which will hit the ground first, and let them go. Repeat the experiment two more times, and record your observations on the data table.

Data Table 1	
Tennis Ball vs. Golf Ball	
Trial 1	
Trial 2	
Trial 3	

Data Table 2	
Tennis Ball vs. Baseball	
Trial 1	
Trial 2	
Trial 3	

Data Table 3	
Ping-Pong Ball vs. Golf Ball	
Trial 1	
Trial 2	
Trial 3	

Data Table 4	
Football Held Sideways vs. Football Held Vertically	
Trial 1	
Trial 2	
Trial 3	

Analysis

1. Which fell faster, the golf ball or the tennis ball?
2. Which fell faster, the tennis ball or the baseball?
3. Which fell faster, the golf ball or the ping-pong ball?
4. Which fell faster, the football held sideways or the one held straight up and down?

 What's Going On?

Back in the late 1500s, Galileo predicted that if gravity was the only force acting on two falling objects, their size, shape, or mass would not affect how fast they would fall. He noted that if two different objects were dropped from the same height at the same time, both would hit the ground at the same time. This prediction was proved in 1971 when *Apollo 15* astronaut David Scott dropped a feather and a hammer side by side on the Moon. Both objects hit the surface at the same time. This experiment would have very different results on Earth, and the reason has nothing to do with gravity. It has to do with air. The Moon does not have an atmosphere, and Earth does. Air resistance, or "drag," affects how fast objects will fall, as well as how well they move horizontally.

In the first two trials, the balls fell at the same speed because they were all round and relatively heavy. The ping-pong ball fell slower than the golf ball because it was much lighter. The force of the air against it was strong enough to slow it down.

Mass is only one factor that controls how air resistance affects the speed of a moving object. Shape also plays a role. The two footballs had the same size and mass, but the football that was held sideways fell a little more slowly. That's because more air pushed against the ball when it was falling. The ball held vertically had a more streamlined shape and could cut through the air more easily.

Our Findings

1. The tennis ball and golf ball should have fallen at the same speed.
2. The baseball and tennis ball should have fallen at the same speed.
3. The golf ball should have fallen faster than the ping-pong ball.
4. The football held sideways should have fallen slightly slower than the football that was held straight up and down.

CAUGHT IN A DRAFT

It turns out that air resistance is a force to be reckoned with in many sports. To reduce the drag caused by air, race cars usually have tapered, bullet-shaped bodies. Bike racers often wear streamlined helmets. One other trick these racers use to beat air resistance is drafting. When an object moves through the air, it pushes air molecules out of the way, creating a small area directly behind it where very little air flows. By getting close behind another racer, a smart racer can take advantage of this "dead air zone" and can save energy.

You can try a simple drafting experiment using a book and a piece of paper. Cut the paper to the same size as the book. Hold the book flat in one hand and the paper flat in the other. Let them drop side by side at the same time. The book will fall fast and the paper will float. Now, hold the book flat in two hands, and place the paper on top. Let the book go. The paper will fall at the same speed as the book. The book is doing all the work; it is pushing the air out of the way. Try the experiment again by holding the paper a centimeter or so above the book, and the same thing will happen. If you hold the paper too far above the book, however, you lose the drafting effect, and the paper will start floating again.

PROJECTILE MOTION

When a quarterback in football makes a long pass, or when an outfielder in baseball makes a throw home, the ball doesn't usually travel in a straight line parallel to the ground. Instead, it moves in an arc. When an object travels in this fashion, scientists say that it follows **projectile** motion. A projectile is any object that is launched and continues in its path of motion due to its own **inertia**. Inertia, as we will discover at the end of this section, is the tendency of an object to continue in its current state, whether that is motion or rest. Projectile motion is the same type of motion that a cannonball or a javelin makes as it flies through the air. In **Experiment 9:** *How the Angle at which an Object Is Thrown Affects Distance*, you will test to see how changing the launch angle of a projectile affects the distance that it can travel.

Like all professional bikers, Lance Armstrong (*above*) wears a streamlined helmet to limit air resistance, or drag. Here, Armstrong bikes during the Amgen Tour of California time trials in Sacramento in February 2009.

How the Angle at which an Object Is Thrown Affects Distance

Topic

How does the angle at which a ball is thrown into the air affect how far it will travel?

Introduction

In some sports—including football, baseball, and basketball—athletes are often required to make long, accurate throws. Several factors control how far an object can travel through the air. One is the speed of the object when it is launched. The harder a ball is thrown, the faster it will leave a person's hand, and the more energy it will have. More energy often means greater travel distance, but not always. In this activity, you will test to see how the angle at which a ball is thrown controls not only its "hang time," but also how far it will travel.

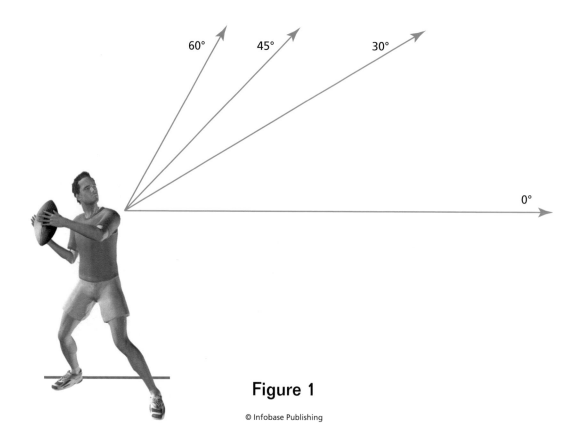

Figure 1

Time Required

45 minutes

Materials

- football
- 3-ft-long (1-m) piece of rope
- football field, soccer field, or similar large, open field
- 3 cones or similar objects to be used as distance markers
- tape measure
- person to assist you

Safety Note This experiment requires that you throw a football a long distance and should not pose a risk to a person who is in good health. No special safety requirements are needed. Please review and follow the safety guidelines.

Procedure

1. Stand at one end of the field. If you are using a field that has goal markings, stand on one goal line. If the field has no markings, stand at one end and stretch out the piece of rope to make a start line. Toss the football back and forth with your partner about 10 times. This will loosen up the muscles in your throwing arm.

2. Stand at the start line and have your partner go out in the field with the cones or other marking devices. Standing flat-footed, you are going to throw the ball as hard as you can. Your partner will use the cones to mark the place that the ball hits the ground. For each trial, you will throw the ball three times. After the third throw, use the tape measure to calculate the distance from the start line for the longest of the three throws, and record the distance on the data table.

3. In the first trial, you are going throw the ball straight out so that when it leaves your hand, it is traveling parallel to the ground. Stretch your arm out so that it is straight out in front of your body. This is the angle that the ball should make with the ground when you release it from your hand. After you have completed the first three throws, measure the longest one and then

have your assistant remove the markers from the field. Rest your arm for a few minutes and then get ready for the next set of throws.

4. In the second trial, you are going to throw the ball at a shallow angle with the ground. Stretch your arm out in front of you again, but this time, instead of holding it parallel to the ground, point it up so that it is about $1/3$ of the way up between the ground and straight up over your head. This is about a 30-degree angle with the ground. Throw the ball at this angle during the second set of passes. After you have completed the second set of throws, measure the longest one, and then have your partner remove the markers from the field. Rest your arm for a few minutes and then get ready for the next set of throws.

5. In the third trial, you are going to throw the ball at a 45-degree angle. Stretch your arm in front of you. Point it so that it is about halfway between being parallel with the ground and straight up and down. This is the angle at which you should throw the ball. After you have completed the third set of throws, measure the longest one, and record it on the data table.

6. In the final trial, you are going to throw the ball at a steep angle with the ground. Stretch your arm out in front of you and point it so that it is about $2/3$ of the way up between the ground and straight up over your head. This is a 60-degree angle with the ground. Throw the ball at this angle three times. After you have completed the final set of throws, measure the longest one and record it on the data table.

Data Table 1	
Distance of Longest Level Throw	
Distance of Longest 30-degree Throw	
Distance of Longest 45-degree Throw	
Distance of Longest 60-degree Throw	

Analysis

1. Why is it important that you throw the ball with the same amount of force during each trial?

2. At which angle did the ball travel the shortest distance?

3. At which angle did the ball travel the longest distance?

4. How did the force of gravity affect the flight of the ball during each trial?

What's Going On?

When you throw a ball through the air, three forces act on it. The first force is your hand, which sends it forward through the air. The second force is air rubbing against the ball, slowing it down. The third force is gravity. While the ball sails through the air, gravity is pulling it down. It is because of gravity that an athlete must put an arc on a ball in order to get it to travel the greatest distance.

Back in the 1500s, Galileo discovered that if you were to drop an object, gravity would pull it straight down to the ground at a predictable rate. If you drop a ball from a height of 33 ft (10 m), it will hit the ground much faster than if you drop the same ball from a height of 3 ft (1 m). The ball dropped from the greater height has to travel a longer distance before it hits the ground, so it has more time to accelerate and build up speed. As it turns out, a ball moving horizontally through the air is affected by gravity the same way and falls toward the ground at the same predictable rate. When you throw a ball parallel to the ground, it has a short distance to fall before it hits the ground. No matter how hard you throw it, the force of gravity will make it hit the ground before it can travel very far.

In order to get the ball to travel the greatest distance, you must make an adjustment to allow for the force of gravity. This means that instead of throwing the ball flat, you must throw the ball up at an angle. This allows the ball to hang in the air for a longer period of time, and it travels a greater distance before hitting the ground. Of course, if you throw the ball at too steep of an angle, it will simply go up and come down. To get the maximum distance, you need to throw a ball at about a 45-degree angle. You can see this any time a quarterback throws a "bomb" to a receiver running the length of the field.

Our Findings

1. The amount of force with which you throw the ball affects its speed, as well as the distance the ball travels.

2. The ball thrown parallel to the ground should have traveled the shortest distance.

3. The ball thrown at a 45-degree angle should have traveled the greatest distance.

4. The force of gravity acted the same on each of the thrown balls.

FUN WITH FRICTION

Friction, like gravity and air resistance, is a force. In fact, air resistance is actually a special type of friction. Simply stated, friction is a force of resistance that acts to slow the motion of an object. Friction can result when an object moves through the air, through water, or when it slides along a surface. The force of friction comes into play in many sports. Depending on the sport, friction can either help an athlete or create major problems. In NASCAR and bike racing, air resistance can be a real drag, but for skydivers and hang gliders, friction with the air helps keep them alive. In **Experiment 10:** *How Shoe Design Affects Friction*, you will discover how different shoes can help athletes get the most out of friction.

EXPERIMENT 10

How Shoe Design Affects Friction

Topic

How does the design of a shoe affect the amount of friction with a surface?

Introduction

Friction can be thought of as the resistance to motion between two objects that are touching and moving past each other. The force of friction plays a role in many daily activities and is critical in many sports. By wearing certain footwear, athletes can control the friction between their feet and the playing surface. In this activity, you will test to see how different footwear produces different amounts of friction, which in turn will affect running time and stopping distance.

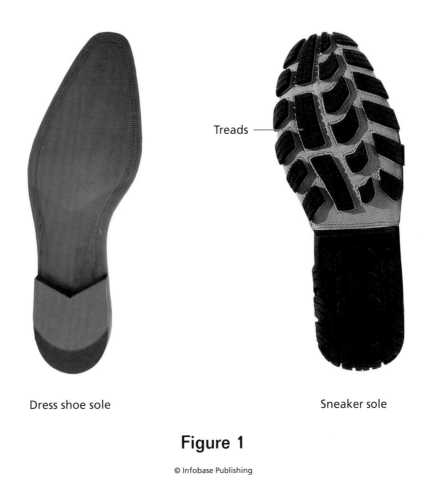

Dress shoe sole   Sneaker sole

Figure 1

Time Required

45 minutes

Materials

- flat grass field, dirt running track, or gymnasium

- sneakers

- shoes with smooth soles (dress shoes)

- stopwatch

- tape measure, yardstick, or meterstick

- 2 pieces of rope, each about 3 ft (1 m) long

- person to assist you

Safety Note This experiment requires that you do moderate exercise and should not pose a risk to a person who is in good health. It is recommended that you conduct this activity under the supervision of a responsible adult. If you have a history of heart or breathing problems, do not do this activity. Make certain that you leave enough distance between the stop line and any obstacles so you don't accidentally crash into them at the end of the run. Please review and follow the safety guidelines.

Procedure

1. If the field that you are using has no markings on it, begin by laying out a running lane. Stretch a piece of rope across one end of the field. This will be the starting line. Use the tape measure to measure a distance of 100 ft (30 m) from the start line, and use the second piece of rope to mark this point. This will be the stopping line. Leave enough distance between the stop line and any obstacles so that you don't accidentally crash into them at the end of your run.

2. In the first trial, you are going to try running and stopping in bare feet. Stretch a few times to warm up your leg muscles. Step up to the starting line and have your partner stand at the stopping line but not behind it. When your partner says "Go," run as fast as you can toward the stop line. Do not attempt to stop until you have reached the stop line. Once you get there,

try to stop as quickly as possible. Stand in place at the point where you stop. Have your partner time how many seconds (to the nearest $1/100th$) it takes you to make the run, and also measure how far beyond the stop line your body came to rest. Record this information on the data table, and then repeat the trial a second time. After you have run the test twice, add your times together and divide by two to get the average running time. Then add the two stopping distances together and divide them by two to get the average stopping distance. Record this information on the data sheet, and rest for a few minutes before you do the next set of trials.

3. Repeat Step 2 wearing the shoes with the smooth soles. Remember to do each trial twice and record all the measurements on the data table.

4. Repeat Step 2 wearing sneakers. Remember to do each trial twice and record all the measurements on the data table.

Data Table 1		
Running in Bare Feet		
Trial 1	Time _____ seconds	Stopping Distance _____
Trial 2	Time _____ seconds	Stopping Distance _____
Total Time = _____ seconds / 2 = Average Time _____		
Total Stopping Distance = _____ / 2 = Average Stopping Distance _____		

Data Table 2		
Running in Smooth-bottomed Shoes		
Trial 1	Time _____ seconds	Stopping Distance _____
Trial 2	Time _____ seconds	Stopping Distance _____
Total Time = _____ seconds / 2 = Average Time _____		
Total Stopping Distance = _____ / 2 = Average Stopping Distance _____		

Data Table 3		
Running in Sneakers		
Trial 1	Time _____ seconds	Stopping Distance _____
Trial 2	Time _____ seconds	Stopping Distance _____
Total Time = _____ seconds / 2 = Average Time _____		
Total Stopping Distance = _____ / 2 = Average Stopping Distance _____		

Analysis

1. Which trial gave you the slowest running time?

2. Which trial gave you the shortest stopping distance?

3. Based on your experiments, why is it a good idea to wear sneakers when playing basketball on a gym floor?

4. Why is it better to wear smooth-soled shoes rather than sneakers when you go dancing?

 ## What's Going On?

Friction is usually thought of as a force that slows objects down, but it also allows us to get moving. When you walk, the friction between the soles of your shoes and the ground propels you forward. If there were no friction, you would not move. When the pavement is wet, or covered with ice, there is less friction between your feet and the ground. Instead of moving forward normally, you slip and slide when you try to walk and keep moving when you try to stop.

In many sports including soccer, track, basketball, and football, athletes wear special footwear to help them get a grip and control their motions on the field or court. The key to controlling friction is the relative roughness of the bottom of the shoe. Basketball sneakers have a series of ridgelike treads like the treads on a car tire. These treads, which are usually made of rubber, are sticky and rough. This increases the friction between the ground and the shoe, allowing an athlete to get a better grip. A better grip means more control over starting, stopping, and turning.

Dress shoes or bowling shoes generally have smooth, flat bottoms. This allows a person to slide easily across the floor. Of course, when athletes play on wet, muddy fields, even sneakers don't have enough friction. In mud or on loose dirt, football, baseball, and soccer players generally wear cleats. These shoes have rubber nubs or metal spikes on their bottoms that literally dig into the ground, giving athletes the grip they need to succeed.

Our Findings

1. Running in smooth-soled shoes usually produces the slowest time.
2. Running in sneakers usually produces the shortest stopping distance.
3. Sneakers work well on gym floors because they allow you to start and stop quickly without slipping.
4. Smooth-soled shoes allow you to slide across the floor and turn more easily, while sneakers tend to stick to the floor.

WAX ON, WAX OFF

As we saw in the previous experiment, too little friction can be a problem for athletes who are trying to maintain their footing on a wet or slippery surface. In some sports, however, the whole idea is to slide over a surface as fast as possible. In ice skating, skiing, snowboarding, and surfing, athletes prepare their equipment in ways that reduce the amount of friction to the absolute minimum. One way to do this is to use a lubricant. Lubricants, such as wax or oil, are designed to reduce friction between surfaces. In **Experiment 11:** *How Lubricant Affects Friction*, you are going to test several lubricants to see which is best at reducing the force of friction between two sliding objects.

EXPERIMENT 11

How Lubricant Affects Friction

Topic

How does the type of lubricant affect the amount of friction between sliding objects?

Introduction

Whenever two objects move past each other, there is a resisting force between them called friction. The force of friction is always opposite the direction of motion. If you were to go to the top of a snow-covered, gentle hill and stand on a pair of skis, the force of gravity will tend to pull you down the hill. If you tried the same thing when the snow was gone, however, you would probably stay at the top of the hill. That's because the surface of the hill without the snow has more friction than the snow-covered hill. The force of friction pushes you up the hill with the same force that gravity is pulling you down. Because the two forces balance, you go nowhere.

Friction happens because every surface, no matter how smooth, is really covered by tiny bumps and grooves. When you try to slide two surfaces past each other, these irregularities grab onto each other. One way to reduce friction between two surfaces is to use a lubricant—a substance that reduces friction when applied as a film between two objects. In this activity, you will test several lubricants on a ramp with a sliding wood block to see which produces the least friction.

Time Required

45 minutes

Materials

- 6-in.-long (15-cm) piece of 2 x 4 wood, or similar-sized wooden block

- thumbtack

- yardstick, meterstick, or large ruler

- flat board at least 4 in. (10 cm) wide and 18 in. (75 cm) long

- bottle of cooking oil

- container of baby powder

- cup filled with water

- paper towels

- medicine dropper

- person to assist you

Procedure

1. Place the wooden block on top of the board at the left-hand side. Push a thumbtack in the top of the block. This side will always be the top side. Slowly lift the side of the board with the block on it to form an inclined plane (ramp) with the bottom of the ramp on the right. Keep raising the ramp until the wooden block begins to slide.

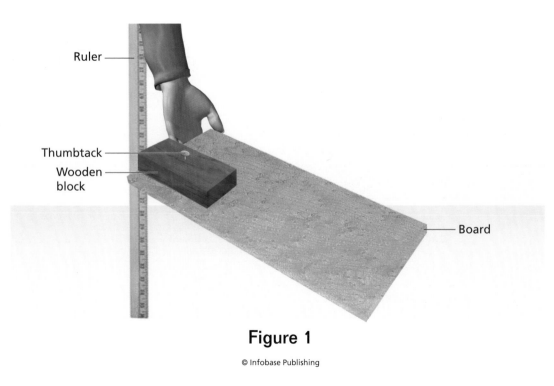

Figure 1

2. Lay the board flat and put the block on top again on the left-hand side. Repeat Step 1, but ask your assistant to hold the ruler next to the left side of the board so that it is pointing straight up. The zero end of the ruler should be resting on the surface next to the board. As you raise the left end of the board, have your friend measure the distance from the surface to the top of the ramp when the block begins to slide down the ramp. Record this figure on the data table, and repeat two more times. Start the block at the same position on the ramp each time. After conducting three trials, add the heights of the ramp together and divide by three. This will give you the average ramp height for the test.

3. Repeat the experiment using the baby powder as a lubricant. First sprinkle an even coating of baby powder on the board. Conduct three trials. Add a bit more baby powder to the board after each trial if you need to. Record your results on the data table, and calculate the average ramp height.

4. Use a damp paper towel to wipe all of the baby powder from the board and block. After the board and block have been cleaned, use the medicine dropper to sprinkle some water drops along the length of the board. Repeat Step 3 using the wet ramp. After each trial, add a few extra drops of water to the ramp. Record your results on the data table, and calculate the average ramp height.

5. Use a dry paper towel to wipe the water off the board and block. Make them as dry as possible. Use the medicine dropper to put some cooking oil along the length of the board. Repeat Step 3 using the oil-covered ramp. After each trial, add a few drops of fresh oil to the ramp. Record your results on the data chart, and calculate the average ramp height.

6. Wipe the oil off the board and block.

Data Table 1	
Sliding Down Bare Wooden Ramp	
Trial 1	Ramp Height _____
Trial 2	Ramp Height _____
Trial 3	Ramp Height _____
Total Ramp Height of All Three trials = _____ / 3 = Average Ramp Height _____	

Data Table 2

Sliding Down Wooden Ramp Covered with Baby Powder

Trial 1	Ramp Height _____
Trial 2	Ramp Height _____
Trial 3	Ramp Height _____
Total Ramp Height of All Three trials =_____ / 3 = Average Ramp Height _____	

Data Table 3

Sliding Down Wet Wooden Ramp

Trial 1	Ramp Height _____
Trial 2	Ramp Height _____
Trial 3	Ramp Height _____
Total Ramp Height of All Three trials =_____ / 3 = Average Ramp Height _____	

Data Table 4

Sliding Down Wooden Ramp Coated in Oil

Trial 1	Ramp Height _____
Trial 2	Ramp Height _____
Trial 3	Ramp Height _____
Total Ramp Height of All Three trials =_____ / 3 = Average Ramp Height _____	

Analysis

1. Based on your results, which surface created the most friction with the wooden block? Which created the least?

2. Based on your results, why do you think it takes a car longer to stop on wet pavement than dry pavement?

3. Why did you conduct three trials and take an average for each trial instead of conducting a single trial to test each lubricant?

 ## What's Going On?

In this experiment, you measured how using a lubricant on a surface reduced friction between the wood block and the surface of the ramp. The steeper the angle of the ramp was, the greater the downward pull of gravity on the wooden block. The more friction there was, the higher you needed to lift the ramp (the steeper the grade) in order to get the block to slide. Each lubricant reduced friction by reducing the roughness of the ramp's surface. Depending how porous the wood of the ramp was, either the baby powder or the oil could have produced the best results. This variability also holds true in sports. Athletes may use different lubricants under different conditions. For example, skiers can choose from a variety of waxes made for wet, soft, powdery, or hard-packed snow.

Our Findings

1. Results will vary, but either the oil or baby powder should have produced the least friction.

2. Stopping a car on a wet pavement is more difficult because the water acts as a lubricant, reducing the friction between the tires and the road.

3. It was important to conduct three trials because using average test results helped to reduce the chance that one trial had some hidden errors in it.

EQUILIBRIUM: A REAL BALANCING ACT

Throughout this section, we have been looking at some of the ways that forces such as gravity, air resistance, and friction play roles in sports. We defined a force as being something that pushes or pulls on an object and causes it to move. The question still remains: Can forces act on an object without making it move? Yes! Just because an object isn't moving doesn't mean that there are no forces acting on it. It simply means that all of the forces are balanced. When the forces acting on an object balance out, scientists say the object is in **equilibrium**.

To see how this works, stand on a bathroom scale and try not to move. While you are standing there, the force of gravity is pulling you down. You know this because your weight registers on the scale. Your weight is controlled by gravity's pull. You are standing still because the scale and the floor beneath it are pushing up on you with a force that equals the force of gravity pulling you down. You don't move because the two forces balance out.

In many sports, athletes have to work hard at maintaining equilibrium. They are always adjusting their bodies in order to stay balanced. To do this, they must adjust something called the **center of gravity**. This point, which is also called the center of mass, is the point in an object at which all the mass appears to be concentrated. If you suspend an object by a string at its center of gravity, it will stay balanced. In **Experiment 2:** *Staying in Balance*, you discovered how feedback systems that are at work in your body help you stay balanced when you run, jump, or bend. In **Experiment 12:** *Testing Your Center of Gravity*, you will see how your ability to balance also involves controlling the forces acting on your body's center of gravity.

EXPERIMENT 12
Testing Your Center of Gravity

Topic

How does changing your center of gravity affect your ability to balance?

Introduction

In sports such as surfing, skiing, and gymnastics, an athlete's ability to stay balanced is extremely important. In order to stay balanced, any object, including a person, must have its center of gravity positioned directly above its point of support. In this experiment you will first locate your own center of gravity and then test to see how changing its position affects your balance.

Time Required

30 minutes

Materials

- room with a carpeted floor
- sturdy chair without arms
- person to assist you

Safety Note   It is recommended that you conduct this activity under the supervision of a responsible adult. If you have a problem with balancing or get dizzy easily, do not do this activity. Please review and follow the safety guidelines.

Procedure

1. Clear out an open space in the room. Place the chair in the middle. Kneel on the floor facing one side of the chair. Slowly move your body forward so that you are lying across the seat of the chair on your stomach. Extend

your arms out in front of you and pick up your legs so that your body is parallel to the floor. (Figure 1 shows how this should look.) You may need an assistant to help you adjust your position. While still lying on the chair, position your body so that you balance on the chair. The point at which you balance is your body's center of gravity.

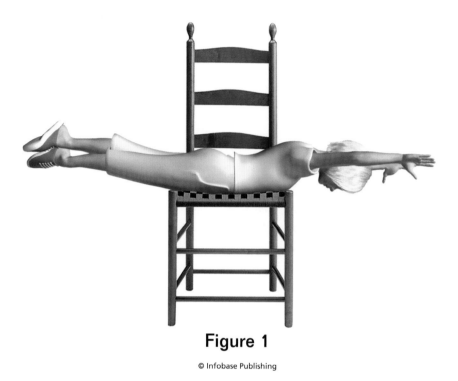

Figure 1

© Infobase Publishing

2. After you have located your center of gravity, stand up and move the chair out of the way. Stand in the middle of the carpeted space with your feet spread about 18 in. (0.5 m) apart. Lift one leg so that you are balancing on one foot. Observe what you need to do in order to stay balanced.

3. Stand on both feet with no space between your feet. Slowly bend forward at the waist. Try to touch your toes without bending your knees. Have your assistant observe your body when you do this, and then have your assistant do it while you observe him or her.

4. Finally, stand against a wall with your feet together with no space between them. The back of your heels should be against the wall. While keeping the back of your legs against the wall, slowly bend forward at the waist. Try to touch your toes again without bending your knees.

Analysis

1. Based on how you balanced while lying across the chair, where is your center of gravity?

2. When you balanced on one foot, what did you have to do to your center of gravity?

3. What happened when you tried to touch your toes while standing against the wall?

 What's Going On?

The center of gravity is defined as the point at which all of the mass of an object appears to be concentrated. If you support an object directly under its center of gravity, it will not shift or rotate. It will balance. If you take a ruler and place it on your outstretched finger, it will balance in the middle. In this case, the center of gravity is also the center of the ruler because the ruler has a uniform size and shape. If you try to balance the ruler by holding your finger under any other point, the ruler will fall off.

For irregularly shaped objects, such as a bowling pin or a football player, the center of gravity is not usually the center of the object. In most people, the center of gravity is about halfway through the body, directly behind the navel (belly button). As long as this point is above a point of support (such as a leg, or an outstretched arm resting on the floor) the person will stay balanced. When you stand on one foot, you naturally shift your center of gravity over the leg that is on the ground.

When you bend to touch your toes, you tend to lean forward because your center of gravity is pushed in front of your body. In order to keep yourself from falling over, you compensate by pushing your rear end backward. This helps to counterbalance the top half of your body. When you try and touch your toes while standing with your back against a wall, you almost always fall forward. That's because the wall keeps you from counterbalancing.

Our Findings

1. If you are like most people, your center of gravity is located about midway through your body directly behind your navel (belly button).

2. In order to stand on one foot, you must shift your body so that your center of gravity is directly over the foot on which you are standing.

3. When you try to bend forward and touch your toes while standing with your back to a wall, you fall over because your center of gravity is no longer over your feet.

UNDERSTANDING INERTIA

Before we conclude this section, we need to revisit the concept of inertia to see how it plays a role in sports. Inertia is the tendency of an object to continue in its current state—whether that is motion or rest. An object at rest will stay at rest and a moving object will keep moving unless there are unbalanced forces acting on it. This idea is one of the most important concepts in science, and it was first described by Sir Isaac Newton. In fact, it is usually referred to as Newton's First Law of Motion. This law helps to explain why everything from hockey pucks to skateboards moves the way it does.

If a football player places the ball on a kicking tee, the ball usually will not move (unless there are strong winds). That's because all of the forces acting on it are balanced. The ball is in equilibrium. If the kicker then kicks the ball, the ball will move because the force supplied by his foot has unbalanced the forces. As we saw in **Experiment 9: *How the Angle at which an Object Is Thrown Affects Distance***, the kicked ball will eventually slow and come to rest on the ground again because of the force of gravity pulling it down and the force of air rubbing against it.

In doing his experiments with inertia, Newton made another important discovery. The more mass an object has, the more inertia it will have. In other words, it takes a lot more force to change the motion of a heavy object than it does to change the motion of a light one. This is one reason that sumo wrestlers and football linemen tend to be large. It is much more difficult for an opponent to move a big, heavy body than it is to move a light one. Of course, less inertia has its advantages in some sports. Sprinters, gymnasts, and high-jumpers tend to be lightweight because then it takes less force to get their bodies moving.

The Spin Is In

Many sports involve something that spins around. Sometimes it's an object that spins, such as a boomerang or a bowling ball. Other times, the athletes themselves do the spinning. Whether it's an ice skater doing a triple axel or track star throwing a discus, rotation plays a major role in sports. When something spins, it has a special type of inertia called **rotational inertia**. Rotational inertia is similar to regular inertia. A bicycle wheel will stay at rest until a force acts on it to make it turn. Once it starts turning, it will keep doing so until another force slows it down. Rotational inertia also is affected by mass. The heavier a turning object is, the more force it will require to either get it going or make it stop.

As you will discover, all moving objects have **momentum**. When objects spin, they also have **angular momentum**. In **Experiment 13:** *How Spinning Wheel Speed Affects Balance,* you will discover how the speed of a turning bicycle wheel affects not only its angular momentum, but also a rider's ability to balance.

EXPERIMENT 13

How Spinning Wheel Speed Affects Balance

Topic

How does the speed of a rotating wheel affect a rider's ability to balance on a bicycle?

Introduction

If you have ever ridden a bicycle, you have probably noticed that it is easier to balance while you are moving. When the wheels of the bicycle are turning, they have a certain amount of angular momentum. This momentum helps keep you balanced. In this activity, you will test how changing the speed of rotation changes the angular momentum of bicycle wheels, which also affects your ability to balance.

Time Required

30 minutes

Materials

- bicycle
- stopwatch or timing device with a second hand
- 2 milk crates
- 2 people to assist you

Safety Note It is recommended that you conduct this activity under the supervision of a responsible adult. Please review and follow the safety guidelines.

Procedure

1. Turn the milk crates upside down. Place one box on each side of the bicycle. With the help of an adult, place the bicycle so that one pedal rests on each box. (Figure 1 shows how this should look.) The front wheel of the bicycle should be off the ground and spin freely. Have the adult hold the frame of the bicycle near the seat to keep it stable and upright.

Figure 1

© Infobase Publishing

2. Push the front wheel so that it turns slowly. Use the stopwatch (timer) to measure how long it takes for the wheel to stop.

3. Give the wheel a hard push so that it turns quickly. Measure how many seconds it spins.

4. Stand in front of the bicycle, facing the front wheel. Grasp the handlebars. Make sure that the front wheel is still. Turn the handlebars slowly back and forth, as if you were turning the bicycle. Note the force required to make the front wheel turn.

5. Repeat Step 4, but have an assistant push the front wheel gently so that it begins spinning slowly. Compare the ease of turning the handlebars to what you experienced in Step 4.

6. Repeat Step 4 again, but have your assistant push the front wheel harder so that it is spinning very quickly. Compare the ease of turning the handlebars to what you experienced in Steps 4 and 5.

Analysis

1. Did the wheel have the greater angular momentum when it was spinning quickly or spinning slowly? How do you know?

2. Was it easier to turn the handlebars when the wheel was spinning quickly or slowly?

3. Based on your observations, how does an object's angular momentum affect its overall stability?

 ## What's Going On?

When an object (such as a bicycle wheel) spins, three factors control its angular momentum: the mass of the object, the speed at which it is rotating, and its radius. Increasing the mass or the speed of rotation will increase the angular momentum. As a wheel turns, it spins around an axis in a certain direction. The more angular momentum it has, the harder it is to make it change direction. This means that trying to turn a fast-spinning bicycle wheel is more difficult than turning one that is spinning slowly. Because a spinning wheel tends to continue in the same direction, the bicycle is less likely to tilt and easier to balance. This is why when an adult teaches a child how to ride a bike, he or she generally gives the child a push to gain some speed.

Our Findings

1. The faster a wheel spins, the greater its angular momentum and the longer it takes to stop turning.

2. It is more difficult to turn the wheel when it is moving quickly than when it is moving slowly or stopped.

3. Spinning objects with more angular momentum are more stable.

FIGURE SKATERS AND HIGH DIVERS

In the previous experiment, you saw that changing the speed of a rotating bicycle wheel changed its angular momentum and its ability to move in a straight line. The radius of a spinning object also affects its angular momentum. This is the distance between the object's center of rotation and the farthest point of rotation. If you were to repeat **Experiment 13:** *How Spinning Wheel Speed Affects Balance* using a wheel with a larger radius, you would find that the wheel would be more stable than a smaller wheel that had the same mass. In many sports, athletes will use subtle moves to change the rotational inertia of their own bodies. In **Experiment 14:** *Testing the Speed of Rotation*, you will discover how changing the position of your own body can have some dramatic effects on the way it spins.

EXPERIMENT 14

Testing the Speed of Rotation

Topic

How does the distance of the mass from the center of gravity affect the speed of rotation of a spinning body?

Introduction

For many athletes, controlling how fast their body spins is a critical part of the sport. Whether it's a figure skater doing a triple axel or a gymnast doing a somersault, the ability to change rotation speed can mean the difference between first place and an honorable mention. When a person spins, his or her body has a certain amount of angular momentum (i.e., the rotational momentum of a rotating body). Angular momentum depends upon the speed of rotation, the body's mass, and the body's radius. The radius is the distance from the center of rotation and the farthest spinning point. In this activity, you will test how changing the radius affects angular momentum by moving some of your body mass in different directions.

Time Required

30 minutes

Materials

- piano stool or similar chair with a rotating seat
- 2 bricks or two 5-lb (2-kg) weights
- clear, open space in the middle of a room
- person to assist you

Procedure

1. Place the piano stool in the clear space. Sit on the stool and draw your legs up under your body so that they are not sticking out or dragging on the floor. (See Figure 1.) Have your assistant spin your body around three times and then let go. Once you are spinning freely, extend your arms. Observe what happens to your speed of rotation. Allow the chair to stop, and then wait a few minutes before moving on to Step 2.

2. Sit on the stool as you did in Step 1. Have your assistant spin you with your arms already extended. After the third spin, have your assistant let go. Once you are spinning freely, draw your arms in toward your body so that you are in the same position that you started in at the beginning of Step 1. Observe what happens to your speed of rotation. Allow the chair to stop, and then wait a few minutes before moving on to Step 3.

Figure 1

© Infobase Publishing

3. Repeat Step 1 and then Step 2. Each time, hold a weight or brick in each hand. Observe what happens to your speed of rotation as you change the position of your arms while holding the weights.

Analysis

1. What happened to your speed of rotation when you extended your arms in Step 1?

2. What happened to your speed of rotation when you brought yours arms in closer to your body in Step 2?

3. How did the added weight affect the speed of rotation in both cases?

4. Based on your tests, if figure skaters want to increase their speed of rotation, what should they do with their body when they begin to spin?

 ## What's Going On?

Once an object begins spinning, it has a certain amount of angular momentum. If there were no external forces, such as friction or air resistance, the angular momentum would not change, and the object would keep spinning forever. In the real world, there are always some frictional forces acting on a spinning system, so eventually the object will come to rest. While the object is spinning, the amount of angular momentum stays fairly constant. Scientists say that the angular momentum is "conserved." Because angular momentum is based on both the speed of rotation and the way the mass is distributed, changing one factor will affect the other. When you extend your arms, you are increasing the radius of rotation. Because the angular momentum stays constant, increasing the radius slows the speed of rotation. The opposite is also true. If you move your arms in closer to your body, you decrease the radius of rotation, and the speed increases. Increasing the mass by adding weights makes the speed change more dramatically.

When a figure skater goes into a spin, there is very little friction to change the amount of angular momentum. The skater increases his or her speed of rotation by drawing his or her arms in close to the body. To slow down, the skater holds his or her arms straight out. You can see this same technique used by high divers. They into a tuck position to spin quickly. When they are about to enter the water, they slow their rotation by extending their legs.

Our Findings

1. Extending the arms slows the speed of rotation.

2. Pulling the arms closer to the body increases the speed of rotation.

3. Adding the extra weight should have had a greater affect on the speed changes.

4. If a figure skater wants to increase speed of rotation, he or she should pull his or her arms in close to the body.

ROTATIONAL INERTIA AND BALANCE BEAMS

Changing rotational inertia not only helps athletes change speed, but also plays an important role in balance. As you discovered earlier, in order for you to balance, you must keep your center of gravity directly above the place that is supporting you. This isn't difficult when you are standing on the floor, but it can be difficult when walking across a balance beam or a log over a stream. Unless you control your motions, you could end up over the edge.

When most people encounter this type of situation, they hold their arms straight out to their sides. Gymnasts will frequently do this when they walk on a balance beam. The reason this helps you balance is rotational inertia. When you are teetering from side to side, you are rotating around your body's center of gravity. By holding your arms out, you are actually moving some body mass away from your center of gravity. This increases your rotational inertia and reduces the speed at which you tilt. In **Experiment 15:** *Throwing a Football*, you will discover how rotational inertia not only keeps a gymnast balanced, but also allows a quarterback to throw a football on target, even on a windy day.

Throwing a Football

Topic

How does the spin of a football affect a passer's ability to throw?

Introduction

In sports such as baseball, tennis, basketball, and soccer, the balls are spherical in shape. Footballs have a different shape. A football tapers to a point at either end, making it much longer than it is wide. This means that a football has a long axis and a short axis. In order to throw a football accurately, a quarterback will usually throw a "spiral." The ball is not only moving forward, but also is spinning around its long axis at the same time. In this activity, you will test and see how spin affects the flight of a football as it moves through the air.

Time Required

30 minutes

Materials

● football

● large, open field

● hard, flat surface (cement sidewalk, wooden floor, or tabletop)

● person to assist you

Safety Note   No special safety requirements are needed. Please review and follow the safety guidelines.

Procedure

1. Place one of the pointed ends of the football on a hard, flat surface. Hold the ball vertically (straight up and down) and let it go. Try to balance the ball on the point.

2. Repeat Step 1, but this time, grasp the ball with both hands and give it a hard twist so that it begins spinning around the long axis. Try to balance the ball on one of the pointed ends while it is spinning.

3. Pick up the ball and stand about 20 ft (6 m) from your assistant. You are going to throw the ball to your assistant two ways. First, throw the ball without any spin. Hold the ball in one hand across its center. The laces should touch all four of your fingertips. When you release the ball, try not to spin it. Repeat this type of throw several more times. With each throw, increase the distance between you and your partner. Observe the way the ball travels through the air.

4. Repeat Step 3, but grasp the ball slightly behind the center. The pinky of your throwing hand should be in the middle of the laces. (See Figure 1.) When you release the ball, twist your wrist so that the ball will rotate around the long axis when you throw it. This should produce a spiral. Repeat the spiral throw several times, increasing the distance between you and your partner each time. Compare the flight of the spiral pass with the way the ball traveled in Step 3.

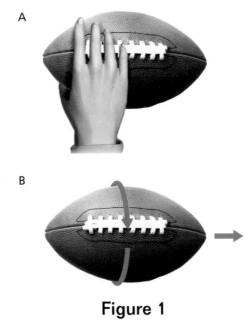

A

B

Figure 1

© Infobase Publishing

Analysis

1. What happened to the ball when you tried to balance it on one point when it was not spinning?

2. What happened to the ball when you spun it and placed it down on one point?

3. How did the flight of the ball in Step 3 compare with the flight of the ball in Step 4?

4. Based on your tests, why is it better for a quarterback to throw a ball with a spiral?

What's Going On?

In order for an object to balance, its center of gravity must be directly in line with the point on which it rests. In the case of a spherical ball, the center of gravity is in the center, so it can be balanced at any point on its surface. Because of a football's unusual shape and the fact that it has laces on one side, its center of gravity is not in the center of the ball. It's slightly off to one side. This makes it easy to balance a football when it is lying flat along its long axis, but when you try to balance it on one of the points, it is almost impossible. This is because when the ball is held vertically (straight up and down), the center of gravity is not in a straight line with the point on which it rests.

When you spin a football around its long axis, however, the ball will balance on the point for a short time. You can see this same effect with a top or a gyroscope. A spinning top balances due to rotational inertia. Inertia is the property of a moving object to maintain its state of motion. As the top (or spinning football) slows down, it loses its rotational inertia and eventually falls over.

Rotational inertia also explains why a football thrown with a spiral can travel straighter and farther than a ball thrown with no spin. As long as the ball is spinning, it resists the tendency to wobble. It will fly straight, even when it is windy. Balls thrown without the rotation tend to float through the air and usually go wherever the wind takes them.

Our Findings

1. When you try to balance a football on one end when it is not spinning, it will fall over.

2. When a football is spinning around its long axis, it will stay balanced on one end as long as it is spinning quickly.

3. In Step 3, the ball should have floated through the air. In Step 4, the ball should have traveled straighter and faster.

4. Throwing a spiral allows a quarterback to throw a football a longer distance with greater accuracy.

WARNING: CURVES AHEAD

As we just learned, when a football quarterback throws a pass, he puts a spin on the ball so it will travel in a straight line. In some sports, however, athletes find it useful to make a ball curve. In baseball, a batter has a harder time hitting a curveball than a pitch that is thrown straight over the plate. In soccer, it's more difficult for a goalie to defend against a "banana ball" than a shot that comes directly at her. When pitcher Johan Santana throws a curveball or soccer star David Beckham bends a ball into a goal, both are using the same scientific principle. In **Experiment 16:** *Testing the Spin of a Spherical Ball*, you will discover how the spin on a ball can really throw an opponent a curve.

Testing the Spin of a Spherical Ball

Topic

How does the spin of a spherical ball affect its path through the air?

Introduction

For many years, a debate raged about whether a curveball actually curved. Some said it did; others said it was an optical illusion. Using high-speed video cameras, scientists showed that curveballs do indeed curve. In fact, a talented pitcher often can make a baseball "break" as much as 18 in. (0.5 m) on its way from the pitcher's mound to home plate. Others balls can take curved paths through the air. Soccer balls, tennis balls, and golf balls also can be made to bend as they travel. The curve happens due to a phenomenon called the Magnus effect, named as such because it was first described by German physicist Heinrich Gustav Magnus. In this activity, you will test the Magnus effect on several different balls to see what makes a curveball curve.

Time Required

30 minutes

Materials

- large, clear, open space in which to throw a ball; the space should be about 15 ft x 15 ft (5 m x 5 m) with no wind.

- soccer ball

- inflatable beach ball

- person to assist you

Procedure

1. Find a clear, open space where you can throw a ball back and forth without hitting any objects. Ideally, you should be inside, far away from any
   fans or blowers that might disturb the air. If you are outside, try to find an
   area where the wind will not affect the flight of the ball.

2. Stand about 15 ft (5 m) from your assistant. Hold the beach ball over
   your head with both hands. Without putting any spin on the ball, throw the
   beach ball to your partner, and observe the flight of the ball. Repeat two
   more times to make sure you get consistent results. Record your results.

3. Repeat Step 2, but when you release the ball, use your right hand to push
   on the right side of the ball and your left hand to pull on it. This should give
   the ball a counterclockwise spin when viewed from above. (Figure 1 shows
   how this should look.) Repeat the throw two more times, and observe the
   path that the ball takes as it travels to your partner. Record your results.

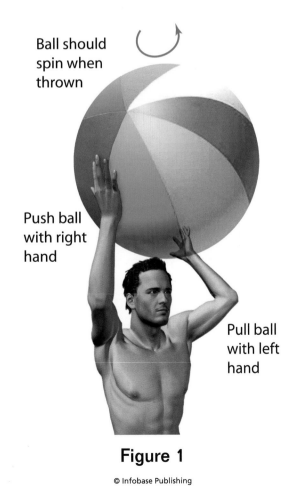

Ball should
spin when
thrown

Push ball
with right
hand

Pull ball
with left
hand

Figure 1

4. Repeat Step 3, but when you release the ball, push with your left hand and pull with your right. Now the ball should have a clockwise spin. Repeat two more times and observe and record the path that the ball takes. Record your results.

5. Repeat Steps 2 to 4 using a soccer ball. Record your observations on the data table.

Analysis

1. What happened to the flight of the beach ball when you threw it without a spin?

2. What happened to the flight of the beach ball when you spun it counterclockwise? Clockwise?

3. How did the flight of the beach ball in Steps 2 through 4 compare with the flight of the soccer ball in Step 4?

4. Based on your tests, if a pitcher wants to throw a curveball that bends to the left, how does he or she have to throw the ball?

 ## What's Going On?

He probably wasn't the first person to recognize it, but in the late 1600s, Sir Isaac Newton noted that the flight of a spinning tennis ball was different than one that had no spin. The spinning ball would follow a curved path, while the ball without spin would travel fairly straight. Newton realized that in order for the ball to change direction, there had to be some force acting on it. In 1853, Heinrich Magnus discovered that a spinning spherical ball affects the air around it as it moves. If the ball is spinning counterclockwise, the air on the right side of the ball gets "dragged" along the ball's surface. It runs into air hitting the front of the ball due to the forward motion of the ball. This collision of air causes the air on the right side of the ball to slow down a little. At the same time, the air on the left side of the ball is moving in the same direction as the on-rushing air, so it speeds up. The difference in wind speed on the right and left sides of the ball results in a difference in air pressure. The pressure is greater on the right side, where the air is moving slower, so the ball is pushed to the left a little. If the ball were spinning clockwise, the opposite would happen. The ball would get pushed to the right.

The amount of curve depends on several factors, including the mass of the ball, its size or surface area, how fast it is moving through the air, and how fast it is spinning. Because the beach ball has a large surface area and very little mass, it will tend to curve more than a soccer ball thrown at the same speed and with the same amount of spin. Because a baseball is fairly small, a pitcher must give it a great deal of spin in order to get a sharp, breaking curve. A talented pitcher can use the Magnus effect to not only make a ball curve to the right or left, but also to get it to break down or up.

Our Findings

1. When you throw a beach ball with no spin, it travels in a straight line.

2. When you throw a beach ball with a counterclockwise spin, its path through the air makes it bend to the left. A clockwise spin makes it bend to the right.

3. When you threw a soccer ball the same way you threw the beach ball, it followed the same patterns, except the curve was not as great.

4. In order to throw a curveball that breaks to the left, a pitcher has to release it with a counterclockwise spin.

STITCHES, LACES, AND DIMPLES

As we saw in the previous two experiments, putting a spin on a ball can have a dramatic effect on the path the ball takes in the air. The shape of the ball plays an important role in how the spin will affect its motion. Yet, the ball's surface texture also is important. A smooth ball, such as a lacrosse ball, will behave differently from one that has stitches, laces, or dimples. Much of this difference is due to the way the air flows around the ball. Stitches on a baseball, laces on a football, and dimples on a golf ball all increase the amount of air resistance (drag) at the surface of a moving ball. Increased drag means that a small change in the motion of the ball can have a large effect on the movement of the air around it. In **Experiment 16:** *Testing the Spin of a Spherical Ball,* you saw that the curve of the ball was due to changes in air speed and pressure acting on the two sides of the ball. These pressure differences were caused by a thin layer of air getting dragged along the surface of the ball as it was spinning. If the ball was perfectly smooth, less air would be dragged along the surface, and the curve would be less pronounced.

A golf ball will fly through the air differently than a smoother ball. The dimples on a golf ball increase the amount of air resistance against its surface as it flies through the air. This makes it easier for the ball to lift up when hit, and it enables the golfer to have more control over the ball.

Actions and Reactions

Without the transfer of energy, sports wouldn't be very exciting. Baseballs wouldn't fly off bats, skateboarders couldn't navigate a half-pipe, and football players couldn't tackle. Energy makes things move, and motion is at the heart of just about every sport. When you throw a Frisbee, kick a soccer ball, or ride a bike, you are transferring energy.

Energy transfer isn't random. There are some rules. One of the first people to describe these rules of motion was Sir Isaac Newton, who was not only a great scientist, but also reportedly an avid tennis player.

NEWTON'S LAWS OF MOTION

Sir Isaac Newton was born in England in 1642, the year that Galileo died. By the time Newton was 30 years old, he was teaching mathematics at Cambridge University and had been elected to the Royal Society of London, where he was already recognized as one of the top scientific minds of his day. In 1685, he began writing the *Principia Mathematica Philosophaie Naturalis,* one of the most important scientific texts ever written. In that book, he described three important rules that control the way things move. Today, these rules are known as Newton's Laws of Motion, and they help to explain why everything—from hockey pucks to racing cars—moves the way it does. In **Experiment 17:** *Applying Newton's Laws of Motion*, you will test to see how Newton's Laws of Motion apply to a person riding a skateboard.

Applying Newton's Laws of Motion

Topic

How do Newton's Laws of Motion affect a person riding a skateboard?

Introduction

In the late 1600s, Sir Isaac Newton described three important rules that help to explain why objects move the way that they do. The first of these rules—called Newton's Laws of Motion—is often called the Law of Inertia. It says that an object at rest will stay at rest or an object in motion will move in a straight line unless an outside force acts on it. The second Law of Motion is called the Law of Acceleration. It says that the rate at which an object changes speed or direction is controlled by both the size of the force acting on the object and the object's mass. The third Law of Motion is called the Law of Action/Reaction. It says that whenever an object exerts a force on a second object, the second object exerts the same force on the first object, but in an opposite direction. In this activity, you are going to test all three Laws of Motion while riding on a skateboard.

Time Required

45 minutes

Materials

- 2 skateboards
- safety helmet and protective padding for two riders
- level, smooth surface on which to ride the skateboards (a gym floor works well)
- tennis ball
- basketball
- person to assist you

Procedure

1. Stand with both feet on the skateboard and have your assistant stand on the ground behind you. Ask your assistant to give you a <u>gentle</u> push, and see how far you roll. Repeat the procedure, but now have your assistant push you a bit harder. Compare the distance you traveled after the first push with the distance traveled after the second push.

2. Have your assistant stand with both feet on one skateboard and face you while you are standing with both feet on the second skateboard. Ask your assistant to <u>gently</u> push against your outstretched hands, and observe what happens. Now have your assistant stand still, and you <u>gently</u> push against his or her outstretched hands. Then, both of you stand on the skateboards and push against each other's hands. (See Figure 1.)

Push apart

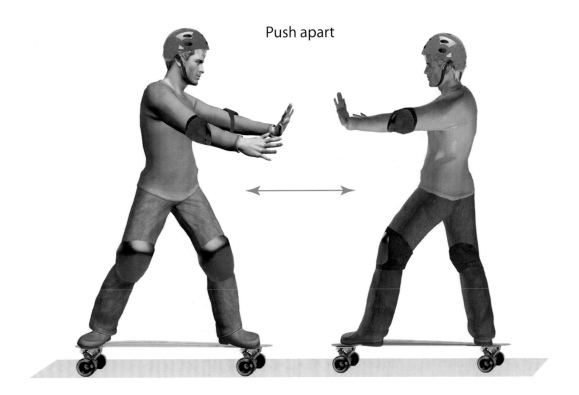

Figure 1

3. Stand with both feet on the skateboard, and have your assistant stand on the ground in front of you about 10 ft (3 m) away. Toss the tennis ball to your assistant while you are standing on the skateboard and observe what happens. Repeat the experiment a second time using the basketball and observe any differences.

Analysis

1. In Step 1, how did the more forceful push affect your motion on the skateboard?
2. What happened when you and your assistant pushed against each other while standing on the skateboards?
3. What happened to your skateboard when you threw the tennis ball and basketball to your assistant?
4. What force caused you to move on the skateboard in Step 3?

 ## What's Going On?

In this activity, you tested all three of Newton's Laws of Motion.

In Step 1, you did not move until your friend pushed you. In other words, because of inertia, your body stayed at rest until a force (the push) made you move. You stopped because friction and air resistance slowed you and the skateboard down. If these forces didn't exist, you and the skateboard would have moved until another force (or an object) stopped you.

When your friend gave you a stronger push in Step 1, you should have traveled a greater distance. You also traveled faster because a larger force acted on you. This follows Newton's second law, which says that a greater force acting on the same object will result in more acceleration.

In Step 2, you and your friend demonstrated Newton's third law. When you were both standing on skateboards, it didn't matter who pushed whom, or if you pushed against each other at the same time. You moved in opposite directions because for every action, there is an equal and opposite reaction. The same thing happened in Step 1, but your friend didn't move because he or she was standing on the ground, and there was a lot of friction. Had your friend been standing on ice, he or she would have slid backward because there would have been less friction.

In Step 3, you experienced all three of Newton's laws again. When you threw the tennis ball forward (the action), you moved backward (the reaction). In this case, the mass of the ball was pushing against you with the same force that you were pushing against it. The ball went farther and faster than you did because its mass was much smaller than yours. Throwing the basketball, which had a greater mass, required a greater force. That moved you a greater distance. In either case, neither you nor the ball moved until an outside force (the throw) was introduced.

Our Findings

1. Increasing the force of your assistant's push should have made you travel a greater distance.

2. When your assistant pushed against you while standing on the skateboard, you should have moved one way while your assistant moved the other way. The same thing should have happened when you pushed against your assistant, and again when you pushed against each other.

3. When you threw the tennis ball while standing on the skateboard, you should have moved backward slightly. When you threw the basketball, you should have moved in the same direction, but farther.

4. When you threw the ball while standing on the skateboard, the force of the ball pushing against you made you move backward.

FOLLOW THE BOUNCING BALL

In the previous experiment, we saw how Newton's three laws explain the way objects move. All three Laws of Motion are important, but when it comes to some sports—such as baseball, tennis, and soccer—the third law (the Law of Action/Reaction) is critical. When a player hits a baseball with a bat or kicks a soccer ball with his or her foot, it causes an action. It is the reaction of the ball leaving the bat or foot that puts the ball into play. Many factors control how a ball will behave when it is hit: how hard it is hit, the angle at which it is hit, and if it has any spin. One of the most important factors has to do with the makeup of the ball itself and its **coefficient of restitution**. A ball's coefficient of restitution is a measure of how well it rebounds or bounces back when it strikes another object. In **Experiment 18:** *Testing a Ball's Ability to Bounce*, you will test how the coefficient of restitution of a tennis ball changes under different environmental conditions.

Testing a Ball's Ability to Bounce

Topic

How do different conditions affect a ball's ability to bounce?

Introduction

When two objects collide, or hit each other, the energy from them has to go somewhere. If you take a ball made out of modeling clay and drop it on a hard floor, the bottom of the ball will flatten. Almost all of the energy of the collision is absorbed by the clay, which changes the shape of the ball. Scientists call this an *inelastic collision.* If you drop a rubber ball on the same floor, it will bounce back up. This is because the ball is made from an elastic material. In an elastic collision, some of the energy of the impact gets "recycled," which causes the ball to bounce. Many sports depend on the consistent "bounciness" of a ball. In this activity, you will test to see how different environmental factors affect the elasticity of a tennis ball when it strikes a hard surface.

Time Required

45 minutes

Materials

- freezer or cooler filled with ice
- handheld hair dryer
- wall next to a floor with a hard surface (wood or concrete)
- yardstick or meterstick
- masking tape
- watch
- new tennis ball
- container of water large enough to fit the tennis ball
- person to assist you

> **Safety Note** No special safety requirements are needed. Please review and follow the safety guidelines.

Procedure

1. Place the yardstick vertically against the wall so that the 0 ft mark is touching the floor and the 3 ft (100 cm) mark is in the air. Use two pieces of masking tape to secure the stick to the wall. It should look like Figure 1.

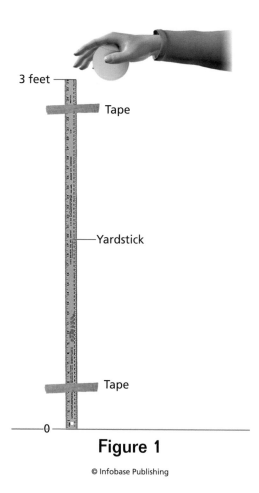

3 feet

Tape

Yardstick

Tape

0

Figure 1

© Infobase Publishing

2. Have your assistant hold the new tennis ball in front of the yardstick. Line it up so that the bottom of the ball is even with the 3 ft (100 cm) mark on the yardstick. Have your assistant drop the ball; remind him or her not to throw it. After the ball hits the floor, use your finger to mark how high the ball bounced back up. Try a few practice drops until you get the hang of it, and then repeat the procedure three times. Record the rebound height of the ball each time on the data table. Add the three rebound heights together, and then divide this number by three to get the average. This number will serve as your "control" measurement against which you will compare your other data.

3. Place the tennis ball on the floor and heat it with the hair dryer for exactly 30 seconds. Repeat Step 2 and record your observations on the data table. Calculate the average rebound height for the hot ball and compare this number to the "control" number.

4. Place the tennis ball in a freezer or cooler filled with ice for 10 minutes. Repeat Step 2. Record your observations on the data table and compare the average rebound height of the cold ball to the "control" number.

5. Let the tennis ball sit on the floor for 10 minutes. Place the tennis ball in the container of water and hold it down so that it is completely covered with water. Hold it there for 15 seconds and then remove it. Allow it to drip into the container for 15 seconds. Then repeat Step 2. Record your observations on the data table. Calculate the average rebound height for the wet ball and compare it to the "control" number.

Data Table 1	
Rebound Height of New Tennis Ball Dropped on the Floor	
Trial 1	Rebound Height _____ in.
Trial 2	Rebound Height _____ in.
Trial 3	Rebound Height _____ in.
Total Rebound Height of All Three Trials = _____in. / 3 = Average Rebound Height _____ in.	

Data Table 2	
Rebound Height of Hot Tennis Ball Dropped on the Floor	
Trial 1	Rebound Height _____ in.
Trial 2	Rebound Height _____ in.
Trial 3	Rebound Height _____ in.
Total Rebound Height of All Three Trials = _____ in. / 3 = Average Rebound Height _____ in.	

Data Table 3	
Rebound Height of Cold Tennis Ball Dropped on the Floor	
Trial 1	Rebound Height _____ in.
Trial 2	Rebound Height _____ in.
Trial 3	Rebound Height _____ in.
Total Rebound Height of All Three Trials = _____ in. / 3 = Average Rebound Height _____ in.	

Data Table 4	
Rebound Height of Wet Tennis Ball Dropped on the Floor	
Trial 1	Rebound Height _____ in.
Trial 2	Rebound Height _____ in.
Trial 3	Rebound Height _____ in.
Total Rebound Height of All Three Trials = _____ in. / 3 = Average Rebound Height _____ in.	

Analysis

1. How did the "control" number compare with the average rebound height of the hot tennis ball?

2. How did the "control" number compare with the average rebound height of the cold tennis ball?

3. How did the "control" number compare with the average rebound height of the wet tennis ball?

4. Based on your observations, how should a tennis player adjust his or her game on a cold, damp day?

What's Going On?

Almost any ball used in a sport will bounce when it is dropped on a hard surface. How much a ball will bounce back is controlled by the way a ball is made and the substance of which it is made. In order for a ball to bounce, it must be elastic. When a ball strikes a hard surface, it briefly changes shape. When the ball returns to its original shape, some of the energy it absorbed in the impact is released. This causes the ball to rebound, or bounce back. In general, the more the surface of a ball deforms, the less bouncy it will be.

When you hold a tennis ball in your hand and squeeze it, you will notice that the surface bends quite easily. This is because a tennis ball is made from a soft rubber core and a felt covering. The center of the ball is filled with air, but because the rubber is completely sealed, the air is trapped in the ball. When a tennis ball gets cold, the air inside the ball contracts, so it does not push with as much force against the rubber around it. As a result, when a cold ball is hit, the rubber will deform more and the ball will not bounce as well. When a tennis ball gets warm, the air inside expands and presses with more force against the rubber. This makes the surface of the ball harder and causes the ball to change shape less when hit. As a result, the warm ball bounces a little higher than the cold ball. When a tennis ball gets wet, the felt covering absorbs some of the moisture. This makes the ball heavier and reduces its ability to change shape. A player using a cold, wet tennis ball will have to hit it harder to get it to travel the same distance as a warm, dry ball would travel.

Our Findings

1. The hot ball should have bounced higher than the control.
2. The cold ball should have bounced lower than the control.
3. The wet ball should have bounced lower than the control.
4. On a cold, damp day, a player would have to hit a ball harder because it will not bounce as well.

PLAYING HARDBALL

Based on the previous experiment, we saw how the amount the surface of a ball deforms helps control how well it will bounce. If you have ever played with a SuperBall, you know that even though it is made of rubber, it has a hard surface that bends very little when you try to squeeze it. A SuperBall has a high coefficient of restitution, compared with a tennis ball or rubber handball. If you try **Experiment 18: *Testing a Ball's Ability to Bounce*** with a SuperBall, you would find that the ball bounces back almost to the starting point on the yardstick. Yet, it will never reach the starting point. That's because no ball, even a SuperBall, has a perfect coefficient of restitution.

When a ball strikes a hard surface, the act of deforming produces some friction. This takes some of the energy away from the ball. In addition, because a ball is usually moving through the air, some of the energy is lost to drag. If you throw a Super-Ball against a concrete sidewalk with a great deal of force, it will bounce extremely high, but that's because you added a great deal of extra energy to it. As it turns out, the same thing will happen with a baseball, even though it's not made of rubber. One of the reasons that a baseball is so hard is so it will travel a long distance when hit. Of course, in order to make a baseball travel a long distance, you have to hit it in just the right way. The action of the bat is just as important as the reaction of the ball. Bats, like balls, come in different sizes and are made of different materials. Each bat has a "sweet spot," and when the ball is hit on this spot, the bat delivers the maximum amount of energy to the ball. In **Experiment 19: *Hitting a Ball on a Baseball Bat's "Sweet Spot,"*** you will test a bat to find its sweet spot and see how it affects the flight of a ball.

EXPERIMENT 19
Hitting a Ball on a Baseball Bat's "Sweet Spot"

Topic

How does hitting a ball on the "sweet spot" of a bat affect its flight?

Introduction

Have you ever watched a baseball game on television when an announcer talks about a player hitting the ball with the "sweet spot" of the bat? This is not just a figure of speech. On every wooden bat is a point off which the ball literally seems to jump. When the ball hits the sweet spot, the sound is unique, too. Instead of a dull thud, there is a characteristic crack, which seems to ring out much louder. In this activity, you will locate the sweet spot of a bat and then test to see if it makes a difference in the flight of a ball.

Time Required

45 minutes

Materials

- wooden baseball bat
- hammer
- baseball
- yardstick or meterstick
- pencil
- wooden utility pole or short flagpole
- person to assist you

Procedure

1. First, find the bat's center of gravity. Stretch your arms in front of you about 18 in. (0.5 m) apart. Stick the pointer fingers of your hands straight out. Ask your assistant to place the bat horizontally across your hands so that it is balanced. Slowly move your hands closer, keeping the bat balanced. When your hands are touching each other and the bat is balanced on top of them, you have located the bat's center of gravity. Use the pencil to mark this point with a dot.

2. Hold the knob of the bat (end of the handle) loosely between two fingers. The bat should hang toward the ground and be free to swing back and forth. (This should look like Figure 1.)

Figure 1

3. Have your assistant begin tapping the bat with the hammer, starting at the thick end of the bat. He or she should work up the length of the bat and then back down again. As your assistant taps, you should feel vibrations in your fingers. When your assistant reaches the sweet spot of the bat, the vibrations should stop. The sweet spot should be very close to the bat's center of gravity. Use the pencil to mark the sweet spot with an "X."

4. Hold the bat straight out in front of you, gripping the handle as if you were going to take a swing. Have your assistant hold the baseball about 18 in. (0.5 m) above the marked sweet spot and drop the ball onto the bat. Observe the ball as it bounces off the bat. Repeat the experiment two more times, and then have your assistant hold the bat while you drop the ball.

5. Repeat Step 4 twice more. First, drop the ball on the fat end of the bat. Second, drop the ball on the handle, near your hands. Observe how the ball bounces off the bat at each location.

6. Stand next to a wooden utility pole or flagpole. Hold the bat in your hands as if you were going to swing at a ball. <u>Gently</u> tap on the pole with the bat. First, tap at the sweet spot, then tap closer to the handle, and then tap at the very end. Compare the way the bat feels in your hands when you tap it on the pole at the different locations.

Analysis

1. How did the sound of the bat change when the hammer hit the sweet spot?

2. How did the ball act when your partner dropped it on the sweet spot, compared with the other locations?

3. How did the bat feel in your hands when you tapped the pole on the sweet spot, compared with the other locations?

4. Based on your observations, why does a baseball player have a better chance of hitting a home run when he or she hits the ball with the sweet spot of the bat?

 ## What's Going On?

A wooden baseball bat is much like the wooden bars on a xylophone. When wood is struck with a hammer, or a ball thrown by a pitcher, it vibrates. Because of its shape, a bat doesn't vibrate the same way along its length. When you get near the center of gravity of the bat, the vibrations are at a minimum. This point is called a "node," and it marks the bat's sweet spot. When a batter hits the ball on the sweet spot, almost all of the energy that is found in the moving bat is transferred to the ball rather than to vibrations in the bat. If a batter misses the sweet spot, much of the energy will be wasted in making the bat vibrate. If a batter misses the sweet spot, the vibrating bat can actually sting his or her hands, especially on a cold day.

Our Findings

1. When you hit the sweet spot on the bat, the bat should ring like a bell.

2. When the ball is dropped on the sweet spot, it should bounce off a little higher than when it hits either end.

3. When you tap on the pole with the bat, the bat should vibrate in your hands at every point except the sweet spot.

4. When a batter hits a ball with the sweet spot of the bat, very little energy is wasted on making the bat vibrate. More of the energy goes into the ball.

A LITTLE LEVERAGE GOES A LONG WAY

Learning to hit a baseball on a bat's sweet spot gives a player a big advantage, but successful hitting also depends on the way the batter holds the bat. That's because a baseball bat is really a **lever**. A lever is a simple machine that allows a person to efficiently transfer energy from one place to another. When a batter swings the bat, the energy from his upper body, arms, and wrists gets passed through the bat and into the ball. Levers are important parts of many tools and devices. The handle of a hammer is a lever, as is a crowbar. A lever works by pivoting at a point called the fulcrum. In sports, athletes use many levers, including hockey sticks, tennis rackets, and golf clubs.

Though it may not look like a baseball bat or a tennis racket, an athlete's leg is one of the most important levers in some sports. When a soccer player kicks a ball, his or her leg is a lever. In **Experiment 20:** *How a Leg Acts Like a Lever,* you will test to see how the human leg works as a lever and the effect of changing the location of a fulcrum on how far a player can kick a ball.

How a Leg Acts Like a Lever

EXPERIMENT 20

Topic

How does a leg behave like a lever when a person kicks a soccer ball?

Introduction

A lever is one of six types of simple machines. All simple machines allow a person to transfer energy from one place to another. In the process, they change the force applied to an object. All levers have two main parts. First, there is a rigid bar that moves back and forth. The bar of the lever is supported by the fulcrum. The fulcrum allows the lever to pivot. It also divides the bar into two arms. (See Figure 1.) The arm that holds the object being moved (called the "load") is the resistance arm. The arm to which you apply the force is called the effort arm. By moving the position of the fulcrum and changing the relative lengths of the two arms, a lever can increase or decrease the amount of force needed to move the load. When a soccer player kicks a ball, the leg acts like a lever. Depending on how the player kicks, the fulcrum can be either the knee or the hip. In this activity, you will test to see how changing the length of a lever arm affects how far a soccer ball will travel when kicked.

Time Required

45 minutes

Materials

- stepladder or plastic milk crate that is sturdy enough to stand on
- 6 ft (2 m) length of 2 x 4 wood, or a board of similar thickness
- 6 in. (15 cm) length of 2 x 4 wood
- soccer ball
- large, open field
- lid from a coffee can

- person to assist you

- 4 small plastic cones or similar objects to be used as distance markers

> **Safety Note**   While no special safety requirements are needed for this activity, it is advised that you conduct it under the supervision of a responsible adult. Please review and follow the safety guidelines.

Procedure

1. Find a level spot in the field, away from windows or other obstructions. Place the short piece of wood at a right angle underneath the long piece of wood to make a simple lever. The short piece of wood will act as the fulcrum, and the long board will be the lever arm. Place the fulcrum directly under the center of the board so that it divides the lever into two arms of equal length. Place the coffee can lid at the end of one arm, and rest the soccer ball on top of it. The lid will keep the ball from rolling off the lever. Place the stepladder or upside down milk crate about 1 ft (30 cm) in front of the other end of the lever. (It should look like Figure 1.)

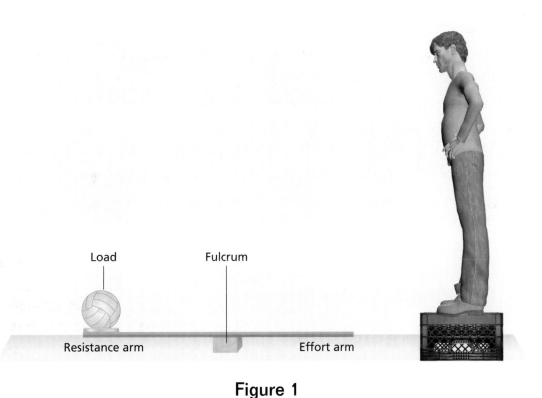

Load   Fulcrum

Resistance arm   Effort arm

Figure 1

© Infobase Publishing

2. Stand on the first step of the ladder or on top of the milk crate. <u>Step</u> (not jump) off the ladder and onto the raised end of the lever. Observe how high the soccer ball goes. Repeat the procedure two more times so that you get consistent results.

3. Reset the lever by changing the position of the fulcrum. Move the small wooden block so that about $2/3$ of the board is now under the soccer ball and $1/3$ of the board is at the end at which you are jumping. Repeat Step 2 and observe any difference in the flight of the soccer ball.

4. Take apart the lever and go to one end of the field with the soccer ball. Ask your assistant to go into the field with the marker cones. Place the soccer ball on the ground in front of you and prepare to kick it. Your assistant will mark the point on the field where the ball comes to a stop. In the first set of trials, you will kick the ball using only the lower part of your leg. In order to do this, you must stand still and bend your leg only at the knee. Kick the ball this way three times and have your assistant mark the distance of all three kicks. After you have completed three attempts, have your assistant remove all but the most distant cone.

5. Repeat Step 4, but keep your entire leg straight and swing your leg from the hip. Compare the distances of these three kicks to the most distant kick in Step 4.

Analysis

1. Did the soccer ball travel higher when the fulcrum was in the middle of the board or when it was closer to you?

2. Did the soccer ball travel farther when you kicked using your entire leg, or when you kicked using your lower leg?

3. When you kicked the ball in Step 4, what part of your leg was the fulcrum?

4. When you kicked the ball in Step 5, what part of your leg was the fulcrum?

5. Based on your observations, what can you say about the length of a lever and the distance a soccer ball travels?

 ## What's Going On?

Levers increase the amount of force that a person can transfer to an object (such as a soccer ball) by increasing the speed at which the object is hit. With a lever, the increase in speed is directly controlled by the position of the fulcrum. When the fulcrum is in the center of the bar, the two arms are equal in length and both ends will move at the same speed, but in opposite directions. When you stepped onto the board with the fulcrum in the center, the soccer ball moved only a small distance into the air. That's because the end of the lever under the ball wasn't moving any faster than the end on which you were jumping.

In order to increase the speed of a lever, you need to move the fulcrum. When you moved the fulcrum away from the soccer ball, you shortened the effort arm of the lever and increased the length of the resistance arm. When you jumped down on the shortened effort arm, it caused the longer resistance arm to move a much greater distance in the same amount of time. This meant that the arm acting on the ball moved faster, and the ball flew a greater distance.

This same explanation holds when a person kicks a soccer ball. When you kick a ball using just your lower leg, the lever is relatively short and moves only a small distance. As a result, there is not as much force on the ball. Kicking from the hip means that your entire leg is acting like the lever. Because you have to move your leg a greater distance, your foot is moving faster when it hits the ball, so it drives it with more force.

Baseball players take advantage of this when they want to hit a ball a long distance. By holding the bat at the end of the handle, they create a long lever that will generate more speed and transfer more energy to the ball. Of course, taking a bigger swing means that it is more difficult to stop the bat. That's why many home-run hitters also tend to strike out a great deal. "Choking up" on a bat handle usually gives a player more control, but the trade-off is that he or she will hit the ball with less force.

Our Findings

1. The ball should have gone higher when the fulcrum was closer to you and the length of the arm under the ball was longer.

2. The ball should have gone farther when you kicked it with your entire leg instead of just the lower leg.

3. When you kicked the ball with your lower leg in Step 4, your knee was acting as the fulcrum of the lever.

4. When you kicked the ball with the entire leg in Step 5, your hip was acting as the fulcrum of the lever.

5. The longer the lever is, the farther the ball will travel.

LITTLE PUSHES THAT ADD UP

Before we close this section on energy transfer, we need to examine one last way in which athletes get things moving in sports. It is called **resonance**. If you think you might have heard this term before when someone was talking about sound, you're correct. Resonance happens whenever energy moves in pulses. It can occur in a vibrating guitar string or in the body of a gymnast working on the rings or parallel bars. It also happens when a diver bounces on a diving board and when a skateboarder builds up speed in a half-pipe. Resonance is all about timing. In **Experiment 21: *How Resonance Affects Motion***, you will discover how a series of well-timed pushes can add up to a whole lot of motion.

German diver Pavlo Rozenberg gets set to dive at the 2009 FINA Swimming World Championships in Rome. A diver bouncing on a diving board uses resonance. A series of well-timed motions—in this case, jumps—adds up to a large amount of force.

EXPERIMENT 21

How Resonance Affects Motion

Topic

How can resonance be used to set an object in motion?

Introduction

Most often, when scientists use the term *resonance*, they are speaking about sound waves and vibrations. Resonance also can be used to explain the motion of objects such as a bridge bouncing up and down when a truck passes over it, or the motion of a child on a swing. Resonance happens when there is an increase in the motion of an object brought about by a series of repetitive forces acting on that object. In order for resonance to work, the external forces have to be timed right.

Resonance comes into play in many different sports. When a diver jumps up and down on a diving board, he or she uses resonance. When a gymnast swings back and forth on the uneven bars, he or she is using resonance. In this activity, you will use resonance to put a softball in motion without hitting or throwing it.

Time Required

30 minutes

Materials

- softball
- 2 wide rubber bands that fit snuggly around the softball
- 18-in. (0.5-m) piece of string
- yardstick or meterstick
- watch that measures seconds
- person to assist you
- 2 6-ft (1.8-m) ladders

> **Safety Note** No special safety requirements are needed for this activity. Please review and follow the safety guidelines.

Procedure

1. Wrap the two rubber bands around the outside of the softball so that they make a cross pattern. Tie one end of the string to the two rubber bands where they cross. Tie the other end around the center of the yardstick. Suspend the yardstick between the tops of the two ladders so that the softball hangs down between the ladders like a pendulum. The softball should be at least 3 ft (1 m) above the ground. (The setup should look like Figure 1.) Note: An alternate approach would be to hang the softball from the center of a doorway.

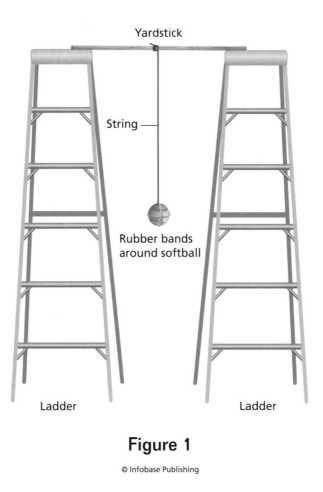

Yardstick

String

Rubber bands around softball

Ladder   Ladder

Figure 1

© Infobase Publishing

2. Allow the softball to come to rest. Put your mouth about 6 in. (15 cm) behind the ball. Blow toward the ball as hard as you can for 15 seconds. Try to blow continuously. After 15 seconds, observe the motion of the ball.

3. Allow the ball to come to rest again. Get in the same position as you did in Step 2. This time, instead of blowing hard against the ball, blow with a small puff once every 3 seconds for a total of 15 seconds. In order to get the timing correct, have your assistant use the watch and say "now" every 3 seconds. Whenever your assistant says "now," blow a puff of air on the ball. Hold your head in the same position the entire time you are blowing. After 15 seconds pass, observe the motion of the ball.

4. Allow the ball to come to rest again. Get in the same position as you did in Step 2. You are going to follow the same procedure as you did in Step 3, except that instead of blowing on the ball every three seconds, only blow on the ball when it comes closest to you on each swing. Have your assistant time you, and after 15 seconds, stop blowing and observe the motion of the ball.

Analysis

1. In which step did the softball move the greatest distance?
2. In which step did you use the most energy?
3. What was different between the way you blew in Steps 3 and 4?

 ## What's Going On?

In this experiment, you demonstrated how a number of small, well-timed forces are more effective at making an object move than a series of high-effort, uncoordinated forces. Each time you blew on the ball, the force of the air made the ball move. In Step 2, you used a great deal of force, but the timing had nothing to do with the movement of the ball. Because the ball was set to swing like a pendulum, when the ball was moving away from you, your pushes were added to the motion of the ball. When the ball was heading toward you, however, you were stopping the ball with your air. The same was true in Step 3; you were blowing at regularly spaced intervals, but the pushes didn't match the frequency of the ball as it swung back and forth. In Step 4, you timed your puffs of air to match the motion of the ball. As a result, all of the little pushes added up to a large amount of force. This is exactly what happens when a parent pushes a child on a swing.

Our Findings

1. If the timing was correct, the softball should have had the largest amount of swing in Step 4.
2. Answers will vary, but you probably used the most energy in Step 2.
3. In Step 3, you blew at a constant rate. In Step 4, you timed your blows to match the swing of the ball.

ROCKING AND ROLLING

Throughout this section, we have looked at how Newton's three Laws of Motion affect the way energy is transferred in different sports. These laws also help to explain why resonance works to make things move.

There is one more experiment that you can try if you are ever at a skateboard park. Go to the bottom of a half-pipe and stand on a skateboard. The board will not move because there are no unbalanced forces acting on you. Because you are at the bottom of the half-pipe, gravity cannot pull you down any farther. This is an example of Newton's first law, the Law of Inertia. Start rocking your hips from side to side. You'll notice that the skateboard will start to move from side to side. Although no outside force is acting on you, your body movements generate a force on the skateboard. When you rock your hips to the right, the board rolls a little to the left. When you rock to the left, the board should move to the right. This is an example of Newton's third law, the Law of Action/Reaction. Because you are at the bottom of a U-shaped track, each time you move to the left or right, you also roll uphill. Then you run out of energy and you roll back down. If you time your hip motions correctly, you can use resonance to begin pushing yourself farther and farther up the slope. Eventually, you will have built up enough energy to do tricks without ever taking your foot off the skateboard.

5

Smash
and Crash

We've already looked at inertia and how an object's mass controls how difficult it is to start it moving. This is the core principle found in Newton's first Law of Motion. Yet, what about the flip side? Does the mass of an object already in motion play a role in how easy it is to make it stop? Before we answer this question, let's take a look at a real-life example from sports.

Let's say you are playing football and you are on defense. You have to stop a player on the opposing team who is blocking for the running back. There are two players coming at you. Both are running at the same speed, but one is 100 pounds heavier than the other. Which player would be more difficult to stop? Even if you have never played or even watched a football game, you probably know the answer. The heavier player would be harder to stop because he has more inertia. Just as a body at rest will stay at rest, a body in motion will stay in motion.

Most often, when scientists speak about inertia in motion, they use the term *momentum*. The momentum of a moving object can be found by taking the mass of an object and multiplying it by its speed or velocity. In **Experiment 22: *How Mass and Velocity Affect Momentum of a Moving Object***, you will put both momentum and inertia to the test by rolling balls with different masses down a ramp at a homemade bowling pin.

How Mass and Velocity Affect Momentum of a Moving Object

Topic

How does changing the mass and velocity of a moving object affect its momentum?

Introduction

Momentum and inertia are linked. Inertia is the resistance of a body to a change in motion, whether that body is moving or at rest. The more massive an object is, the more inertia it has. Momentum exists only for moving objects. It can be thought of as "moving inertia." Momentum is the product of the mass of a moving object and its velocity. The more momentum a moving object has, the harder it is to change its motion. In this activity, you are going to test how changing the mass of a stationary object affects its inertia and how changing both the mass and the velocity of a moving object controls its momentum.

Time Required

45 minutes

Materials

- softball
- basketball
- 2-liter soda bottle with cap
- water
- five thick textbooks, wooden blocks, or bricks
- wooden board about 4-ft-long (120 cm) and 1-ft-wide (30 cm) to serve as ramp

> **Safety Note**   No special safety requirements are needed for this activity.
> Please review and follow the safety guidelines.

Procedure

1. Prop up one end of the large wooden board on two thick books, wooden blocks, or bricks so that you have a ramp. Place the empty soda bottle at the bottom of the ramp. (The setup should look like Figure 1.)

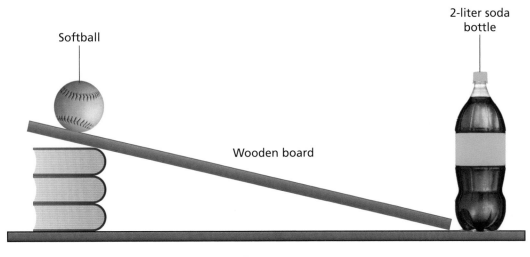

Softball

2-liter soda bottle

Wooden board

Figure 1

© Infobase Publishing

2. Place the softball at the top of the ramp. Line it up so that it will hit the bottle when it rolls down the ramp. Release the softball and observe what happens to the bottle when the ball hits it.

3. Fill the bottle with water. Screw the cap on tightly. Repeat Step 2 with the softball and observe what happens when the ball hits the full bottle.

4. Repeat Step 2 using the basketball. Observe what happens to the bottle when the basketball hits it.

5. Place two more books, blocks, or bricks under the raised end of the board so that you double the height of the ramp. Repeat Step 2 with the softball on the raised ramp, and observe what happens to the motion of the ball and what happens to the bottle when the ball hits it. Compare this to what happened in Step 4.

6. Repeat Step 5 using the basketball. Before you do, predict what will happen to the motion of the basketball and what will happen to the bottle when the ball hits it.

Analysis

1. What happened to the empty bottle when the softball hit it?

2. What happened to the full bottle when the softball hit it in Step 3?

3. What happened to the inertia of the bottle when you filled it with water? How do you know?

4. What happened to the full bottle when the basketball hit it in Step 4?

5. Which ball had the greater momentum, the softball in Step 3 or the basketball in Step 4? How do you know?

6. What happened to the speed of the softball when you raised the ramp? How did this affect its momentum? How do you know?

 ## What's Going On?

In this experiment, you demonstrated the fact that both momentum and inertia are affected by mass. When the soda bottle was empty, it was easily knocked over by the rolling ball. Once the bottle was filled with water, it gained inertia because it had much more mass. The softball rolling down the same ramp could not move it as much as it did the empty bottle.

Both the softball and the basketball had momentum when they rolled down the ramp. In Steps 3 and 4, the basketball and the softball had the same speed when they reached the bottom of the ramp. Because the basketball had more mass, it also had more momentum. That is why the basketball could easily knock over the full water bottle but the softball couldn't. By raising the ramp, you increased the speed at which the balls rolled down it. Increasing the speed of the softball gave it more momentum, so it moved the full bottle more in Step 5 than in Step 3. Because momentum is the product of both mass and velocity increasing, either of these will increase the momentum.

Our Findings

1. The empty bottle should have tipped over when the softball hit it.

2. The full bottle might have tipped a little, but it should have remained standing when the softball hit it in Step 3.

3. Filling the bottle with water increased its inertia because it increased its mass. You can tell that the inertia increased because the softball could not knock over the full bottle.

4. The basketball should have knocked over the full bottle.

5. The basketball had more momentum than the softball. The basketball knocked over the full bottle, but the softball didn't.

6. Raising the ramp increased the speed of the softball. Increasing the speed also increased the momentum because when the softball hit the full bottle in Step 5, the bottle moved more.

CHANGING MOMENTUM

Momentum is a word that is used a great deal in sports. Often when a team makes a big score, an announcer will say that there has been a "shift in momentum" in the game. This use of the word may not fit the scientific definition of the term, but it does give you a sense of how important momentum is. When the momentum of a game changes, there is a major shift in who is doing well. Changing the momentum of a moving object also produces a shift in its speed or direction. Changing the momentum of a moving object doesn't happen all by itself. It takes a force. A force acts on an object over a period of time. When scientists measure the length of time that a force acts on an object, they refer to that time as an **impulse**. In **Experiment 23: *Changing the Impulse of a Force on a Soccer Ball***, you'll discover how changing the impulse can have a dramatic effect on the flight of a soccer ball.

EXPERIMENT 23

Changing the Impulse of a Force on a Soccer Ball

Topic

How does changing the impulse of a force affect the distance a soccer ball travels?

Introduction

When forces act on an object, they usually do so over a period of time. The longer a force acts on an object, the larger the total force will be. When scientists measure the amount of time that a force acts on an object, they use the term *impulse.* In this activity, you will test how changing the impulse on a soccer ball affects how far it travels.

Time Required

30 minutes

Materials

- soccer ball or kick ball

- large, open field

- measuring tape

- 4 plastic cones or similar object to mark distance

- person to assist you

Safety Note   No special safety requirements are needed for this activity. **Please review and follow the safety guidelines.**

Procedure

1. Take the soccer ball and one of the distance markers to one end of the field. Have your assistant go to the other end of the field with three of the distance markers. Select a point at your end of the field to be the starting line and place the marker you were carrying there.

2. Place the soccer ball on the ground next to the marker. In the first trial, you are going to kick the ball with an impulse of a short duration. Stand with both feet flat on the ground. Bring your kicking leg back as far as it will go and then swing it forward to kick. <u>Don't run or jump first.</u> When you bring your foot forward, stop its motion as soon as it hits the ball. <u>Do not swing your leg past the ball.</u> Your assistant will mark the place that the ball comes to rest with one of the cones. Repeat this procedure two more times. Use the tape to measure the distance to each cone and record this information on the data table. Add the three distances together and divide by three to get the average distance that you kicked the ball. Have your assistant collect the distance markers.

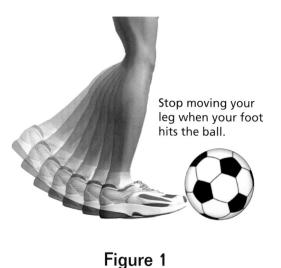

Stop moving your leg when your foot hits the ball.

Figure 1

© Infobase Publishing

3. Repeat Step 2, but when you make contact with the ball, continue swinging your leg forward. In other words, follow through with your kick. This will produce an impulse of a longer duration. When you kick the ball, try to use the same amount of force that you did in Step 2. After you complete three kicks, record your measurements on the data table.

Analysis

1. Did the ball travel a longer distance in Step 2 or Step 3?

2. In which step did your foot touch the ball for a longer period of time?

3. In which step did you kick the ball harder?

Data Table 1	
Distance the Soccer Ball Traveled with a Short Impulse Kick	
Trial 1	
Trial 2	
Trial 3	
Total Distance of All Three Trials = _____ / 3 = Average Distance Traveled _____	

Data Table 2	
Distance the Soccer Ball Traveled with a Long Impulse Kick	
Trial 1	
Trial 2	
Trial 3	
Total Distance of All Three Trials = _____ / 3 = Average Distance Traveled _____	

 What's Going On?

You often will hear coaches tell players to "follow through" when they hit, kick, or throw a ball. It doesn't matter if they are playing baseball, tennis, golf, or soccer. When you follow through, you are allowing the force to act on the ball for a longer period of time. In other words, the impulse is of a longer duration. The longer the force acts, the greater the total force will be, and the faster the ball will travel. When you kicked the ball in Step 2, you did not follow through. Instead, you stopped your leg, which made the impulse short. This meant that the force acted for a short time, so the total force on the ball wasn't very large. In Step 3, you continued your leg moving through the ball. This allowed your foot to stay in contact with the ball for a greater period of time, making the impulse longer.

Our Findings

1. The soccer ball should have traveled a greater distance in Step 3.

2. Your foot stayed in contact with the ball for a longer period of time in Step 3.

3. Because of the way you were standing, the strength of your kick should have been the same for both trials even though the results were different.

SUDDEN IMPACTS

In the previous experiment, we saw how increasing the length of time on which a force is applied increases the total amount of force acting on an object. When a pitcher winds up before throwing a baseball, he is using this technique to help increase the speed of the ball. Yet, spreading a force out over a longer duration can have the opposite effect. In fact, this is what keeps you from being injured when you high dive into the water.

Many people believe that people aren't injured when they dive into a pool because the water is "soft." That's not the entire story. A person can land in water without getting injured because water spreads the force of impact over a long period of time. When you hit the water, you don't stop. Instead, your momentum is gradually reduced as you sink. It is another case of changing the impulse of the force. In **Experiment 24: *The Force of Colliding Objects***, you will use this same technique to decrease the force acting on a falling body.

When objects collide, the force of impact is affected by the length of time over which the collision takes place. When a person dives into water, the water spreads the force of impact as the person's momentum gradually decreases with the action of diving deeper into the pool.

The Force of Colliding Objects

Topic

How does changing the length of time that a collision occurs affect the amount of force acting on the colliding objects?

Introduction

When objects collide, the length of time over which the collision takes place directly affects the force of impact. When scientists measure the amount of time that a force acts on an object, they use the term *impulse.* In this activity, you will test how changing the impulse of a collision affects the force of a softball's impact as it hits a sheet of newspaper.

Time Required

30 minutes

Materials

- softball

- 6 sheets of newsprint, all from the same newspaper with no rips or tears

- sturdy chair or stepladder

- yardstick or meterstick

- 3 people to assist you

Procedure

1. Stand on the chair or ladder. Hold a softball in one hand and stretch that arm out in front of you. Your outstretched hand should be about (6 ft) 2 m above the ground. Have two assistants kneel on the floor below you. Ask them to take a sheet of newspaper and stretch it horizontally (flat) about 3 ft (1 m) below the softball. Have a third assistant check the distance using the yardstick.

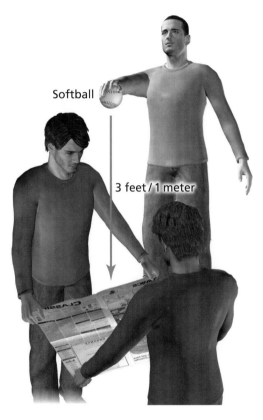

Softball

3 feet / 1 meter

Figure 1

© Infobase Publishing

2. Ask your assistants to hold the newspaper so that it is stretched tight, but not so tight that it rips. There should be no wrinkles on the surface. Position your hand so that the softball is directly over the center of the newspaper. Drop the softball. Do not throw it. Observe what happens when the softball strikes the newspaper. Repeat the procedure two more times to see if you get the same result.

3. Repeat Step 2, but ask your assistants to hold the newspaper loosely so that it sags 1.5 in. (about 4 cm) in the middle. Use the yardstick to make sure you drop the ball from the same height above the newspaper as you did in Step 2. Observe what happens when the softball hits the newspaper. Repeat the procedure two more times to see if you get the same results.

Analysis

1. What happened to the tightly stretched sheet of newspaper when the ball hit it?
2. What happened to the loosely held newspaper when the ball hit it?
3. In which trial did the impact of the ball take longer?

 ## What's Going On?

In this experiment, the falling softball had a certain amount of momentum when it hit the newspaper. When the newspaper was stretched tight, the ball probably ripped right through it. When the paper was held loosely, the ball probably came to rest on top of the paper. When the paper was stretched tight, there was no "give" in the paper. When the ball hit, the force of the impact happened quickly. The loosely held paper could flex in response to the force of the falling ball. The ball fell with the same amount of force in both trials, but in the second trial, the force was spread over a longer period of time. As a result, the paper was able to absorb the impact without tearing.

You can see this same thing in a baseball game. When a catcher or first baseman "sets up" to receive a throw, he usually stretches out his gloved hand. When the ball arrives, he will then pull his arm back toward his body. This spreads the force of the ball's impact over a longer time period and reduces the effect on the player's hand inside the mitt.

Our Findings

1. When the paper was held tight, the ball should have ripped through it.
2. When the paper was held loosely, the ball should have come to rest on the paper without tearing it.
3. When the paper was held loosely, the duration of the impact was longer.

AIR BAGS AND BUNGEE CORDS

If you have ever watched a track-and-field competition, you've probably noticed that athletes who participate in the high jump and pole vault land on large air bags. When they hit the bag, it is designed to slowly collapse under them. This increases the length of time that the force of impact acts on their bodies. By spreading out the force over a longer period of time, the impact on a person's body is reduced. Stunt people also use air bags when they jump out of buildings, but modern technology has given them one other important tool—the decelerator. A decelerator is the opposite of an accelerator. Instead of speeding up a person, it slows a person down. The use of decelerators has also led to another interesting sport called bungee jumping.

A bungee cord is like a rope, but much more elastic. When a force is applied to a bungee cord, it will stretch well beyond its starting length. When a bungee jumper first jumps, the cord tied to his feet starts off slack. As the jumper falls through the air, he quickly gains speed due to acceleration from the force of gravity. As we saw in **Experiment 21: *How Resonance Affects Motion***, an increase in speed also produces an increase in momentum. Eventually, the jumper reaches the end of the bungee cord. If the bungee cord acted like a typical rope or cable, it would bring the jumper to a sudden halt. This would probably result in severe damage to his legs and spine. Instead, the bungee cord stretches. As it stretches, his speed slowly decreases until he finally comes to a stop, hopefully well before he hits the ground!

Unlike a typical rope or cable, a bungee cord is made to stretch so that a person does not come to a sudden halt. This spreads out the force over a longer period of time and, therefore, reduces the impact on the person's body.

PADDING WITH A PURPOSE

Scientists and athletes alike are always in search of new and improved ways of reducing the impact from sports collisions. One way to soften the blow is through the use of padding. In some sports, such as football and hockey, players must wear a great deal of protective gear. In sports such as volleyball and skateboarding, pads are usually worn only on specific body parts. Protective gear has benefits, but it also can create some problems. Hockey masks and football helmets can block a player's view. Padding on the arms and legs can restrict an athlete's ability to move. To be truly effective, good protective gear must maximize the level of protection and minimize bulk. This is particularly true for the football helmets. In **Experiment 25: *Testing Safety Helmet Materials***, you will discover why modern football helmets are designed the way they are. You will test several materials to see which combination offers the best protection for a raw egg.

EXPERIMENT 25 — Testing Safety Helmet Materials

Topic

What combination of materials makes the most effective safety covering?

Introduction

Athletes use many different types of protective gear. One of the most important is the safety helmet, which covers and protects an athlete's head. Helmets are seen in football, baseball, hockey, bicycle racing, skiing, and skateboarding. To be truly effective, a safety helmet has to be lightweight but strong. It has to withstand powerful impacts on the outside, yet it must not transmit the force of an impact to the player's head on the inside. In this activity, you will test several materials to see which combination makes the most effective safety helmet.

Time Required

60 minutes

Materials

- 2 disposable 8-oz hard plastic cups
- 4 raw eggs
- floor with a hard surface
- plastic drop cloth
- roll of paper towels
- roll of masking tape
- yardstick or meterstick
- person to assist you

Safety Note While no special safety requirements are needed for this activity, it is advised that you conduct it under the supervision of a responsible adult. Please review and follow the safety guidelines.

Procedure

1. Spread out the plastic drop cloth over a floor with a hard surface (concrete or hard wood works best). Stand in the middle of the drop cloth and stretch your arm out. Have your assistant measure the height of your arm above the floor. It should be exactly 3 ft (1 m) above the ground. This is the height from which you will drop your eggs.

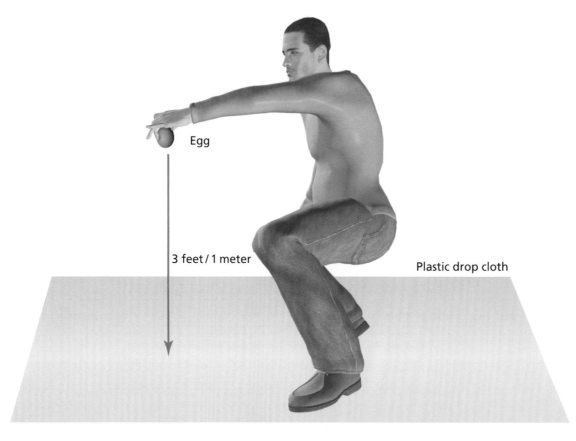

Egg

3 feet / 1 meter

Plastic drop cloth

Figure 1

© Infobase Publishing

2. Hold a raw egg in your outstretched hand and let it drop to the floor. The egg should break on impact. This egg will serve as the control. It shows what would happen to an egg when no protective covering is used.

3. Take another egg and place it inside one of the plastic cups. Put two pieces of masking tape over the open end of the cup to keep the egg from falling out. Hold the cup right-side up, 3 ft (1 m) above the floor. Let it fall. Observe what happens to the egg in the cup.

4. Completely wrap another egg with the paper towel. Secure the towel to the egg using a piece of masking tape. Hold the egg at the same height as you did in Steps 2 and 3 and let it fall. Observe what happens to the egg.

5. Wrap the final egg in a paper towel, but do not tape the towel to the egg. Instead, place the towel-wrapped egg inside the second plastic cup. Place two pieces of tape over the end of the cup. Hold the cup right-side up at the proper height. Let it fall. Observe what happens to the egg in the cup.

Analysis

1. What happened to the bare egg in the plastic cup when it hit the ground?

2. What happened to the egg wrapped in only the paper towel when it hit the ground?

3. What happened to the egg wrapped in the paper towel and placed inside a cup when it hit the ground?

 ## What's Going On?

Helmets are used to protect players from serious head injuries, including skull fractures and concussions. In this experiment, the egg was used to represent a player's head. The egg received the best protection from a combination of materials set in layers around it. This is the same design that a modern football helmet uses, except the materials are a little more high tech. To be truly effective, a helmet must be able to receive a blow without breaking and also absorb the energy of impact without transmitting it to the player's head inside.

Modern football helmets are made of three different layers. The outermost shell is usually a rigid type of plastic known as a polycarbonate alloy. It is dome-shaped, which helps to transmit the force of the impact around the outside of the helmet. Inside the helmet is a padded liner made from foam rubber. This is designed to soften the blow to the player's head. Most modern football helmets also contain an air bladder, a balloonlike device that can be inflated and deflated until the helmet properly fits the player's head. When a player gets hit, the air bladder compresses. This increases the amount of time that the force is applied, reducing the severity of the blow.

Our Findings

1. The egg in the cup alone should have cracked on impact.

2. The egg wrapped in the paper towel alone should have cracked on impact.

3. The egg wrapped in the paper towel and placed inside the cup should have showed the least amount of damage.

A BRIEF HISTORY OF FOOTBALL HELMETS

If you have ever played tackle football or watched the game up close, it is hard to believe that anyone would play without a helmet. But, for many years, that was how it was played. Protective headgear did not become mandatory in the National Football League until the mid-1940s. Before that time, helmets were optional, and many players tried unique ways to protect their noggins.

No one really knows who first came up with the idea of wearing a helmet. In the late 1890s, some players began experimenting with head coverings made from leather and moleskin. These early designs did almost nothing to protect the head from impact. They were worn to protect a player's ears from damage.

Around 1920, football helmets started to become more standardized. They were still made of leather and were similar in design to the headgear that pilots wore during World War I. These newer helmets had a hard leather top that was round instead of flat. The round design helped to spread the impact of blows to the top of the head. Also at about this time, the first fabric liners were being placed inside helmets to help absorb shock.

The first modern football helmet was introduced in 1939 by the Riddell Company. It was made from an early form of plastic. Past helmets had been fastened around a player's neck. This one used a chinstrap. The face mask was introduced in the 1940s. It helped to reduce injuries to a player's nose and teeth.

Football helmets have come a long way since the earlier models, such as the helmet being worn by American football player and coach Knute Rockne, seen here in the 1920s.

6

Technology and the Future of Sports

Over the years, scientists have played many important roles in sports. As you read previously, by studying the human body and how different body systems function, biologists have developed athletic training techniques to make athletes stronger and faster. In addition, thanks to a better understanding of how the body breaks down and uses food, nutritionists have created sports-specific diets that provide more energy and endurance. This allows athletes to compete harder and train longer.

When it comes to sports medicine, trainers using the latest biomechanics information can work with athletes to reduce the risk of injury. When injuries do happen, surgeons can repair joint or muscle damage that would have ended many athletes' careers in the past. After surgery, physical therapists have reduced recovery times from years to months.

Improving, protecting, and rehabilitating injured athletes is important. Still, it is far from the only role that scientists play in sports. Almost every day, material scientists and engineers make scientific breakthroughs that eventually lead to new and improved sports equipment. Everything from faster racing bikes to better running shoes can be traced to a scientific discovery. Here are just a few recent technological developments in sports that have their roots in science.

HIGH-TECH HELMETS

As we saw in the previous unit, football helmets have come a long way since they were first made out of moleskin and leather. One of the most important innovations happened in the early 1970s, when scientists first put an inflatable air bladder inside the helmet. Today, these devices are standard in most of the helmets used by professional, college, and even high school football players.

Even with air bladders in their helmets, football players still run a high risk of head injuries, especially concussions. In the 1990s, researchers working in labs and using video analysis of players in games discovered that more often than not, a concussion-causing impact was on the side of the player's head, not the top. Using this new information, engineers at the Riddell Company, with the help of computers, redesigned the shape of the football helmet. They took the center of gravity of the human head into consideration. In 2002, they released a new helmet called the Revolution.

Scientists at the University of Pittsburgh Medical Center conducted a three-year study of more than 2,000 high school football players who used this new helmet while competing in games. Compared with players wearing traditional helmets, players wearing the Revolution has about a third fewer concussions. This was a big improvement, but it did not eliminate the risk. Even with the new and improved helmets, the Brain Injury Association of America estimates that about 250,000 football players will sustain some type of head injury each year. This is where HITS is designed to help.

HITS stands for Head Impact Telemetry System. It consists of six sensors and a microprocessor that fit inside a player's helmet, along with a battery and a radio transmitter. The sensors are inside the padding of the helmet. They can detect the magnitude, direction, and duration of up to 100 impacts. The entire package weighs about 6 oz. It transmits data to a computer on the sidelines. Ideally, when a player takes a blow to the head, the coaching staff can use HITS data to see how severe it is. Coaches can then check on the player to see if he or she needs additional medical attention. The HITS isn't designed to diagnose concussions, but it may eventually be used to help engineers design even safer football helmets.

NASA SWIMSUITS

When it comes to breaking world records, every little bit helps. As you previously read, one of the biggest challenges faced by racing athletes is friction, or drag. On the ground, wind resis-

The high-tech Speedo LZR, worn by swimmer Michael Phelps (*center*) during the 2008 Olympics, tightly compresses the body to reduce drag and is made with a fabric that produces less friction during swimming. Phelps models the suit, which has since been banned, here in 2008 along with swimmers (*from left*) Ryan Lochte, Katie Hoff, Amanda Beard, Natalie Coughlin, Kate Ziegler, and Dara Torres.

tance is caused by moving air currents. In a pool, the drag is caused by water. Over the years, swimmers have tried many techniques to reduce drag, including shaving their body hair and spreading oil on their skin. With the help of some real rocket scientists, however, it appears that swimmers finally might have a breakthrough.

During the 2008 Summer Olympic Games in Beijing, swimming records were shattered on a near-daily basis. Most of the credit still goes to the athletes themselves, but many people believe that the record-breaking pace was helped by a high-tech Speedo swimsuit called the Speedo LZR. Swimmer Michael Phelps wore one when he won eight gold medals during the games. The suits—now banned from international swimming competitions—were so tight that they actually compressed the body. The compression reduces any "jiggling" due to loose skin that would normally be in direct contact with the water, and the suit's fabric provides less friction than bare skin does as a swimmer moves through the water.

The materials used in the Speedo LZR suits were tested by aerospace engineer Steve Wilkinson using the low-speed wind tunnel at NASA's Langley Research facility in Hampton, Virginia. Most of the time, Wilkinson uses the device to test the drag coefficients of materials used in planes, boats, and rockets.

In the same way that reducing friction with the air helps planes fly more efficiently, reducing friction with the water helps an athlete swim faster. Studies had shown that almost one-third of the force acting against a swimmer in the water comes from friction with the skin, so identifying a fabric that was smoother than skin would pay big dividends.

Wilkinson tested almost 60 different fabrics and weave patterns. He sent the data to researchers on Speedo's Aqualab development team. They eventually wove the winning fabric into a suit. Of course, having a high-tech swim suit isn't going to guarantee a victory. The swimmer has to be great, too. Still, in a race that is often decided by hundredths of a second, every little bit helps!

BUILDING A BETTER BIKE

Swimsuits aren't the only pieces of sports equipment that have undergone wind-tunnel tests. In an attempt to give bicycle racers an edge over their opponents, scientists and engineers use large-scale wind tunnels to test the effects of drag on just about every part of a racing bike—from the handlebars and wheels to the water bottle and the rider's helmet. Each of these special wind tunnels has a floor that acts like supersensitive balance scale. The floor picks up the slightest movement of an object on top of it. Most often, the bicycle is secured to the floor with two large struts. When the blowers are turned on, sensors pick up any motion by the bike and send it to a computer. By changing the direction and speed of the wind, researchers can get a full profile of how the bike and rider will react to drag under a variety of conditions.

Based on these tunnel tests, researchers have found that less than one-third of the drag on a bicycle racer comes from the bike itself. Most of the air resistance comes from what the rider is wearing and his or her position on the bike. Test data has shown that the way a rider places his or her shoulders, forearms, hands, and even thumbs can make a big difference in the overall drag. Just like the space-age swimsuits, bicycle racers often wear tight "skinsuits" and aerodynamically designed helmets to minimize friction.

CHANGING THE SHAPE OF SOCCER BALLS

As previously discussed, laces, dimples, and stitches can dramatically alter the path of a ball as it moves through the air. The manufacturers of soccer balls know this fact well. In 2006,

Adidas, which is the world's largest producer of soccer balls, introduced a new ball design called the +Teamgeist for use in the World Cup soccer tournament. A traditional soccer ball has a pattern of 32 alternating black and white hexagons and pentagons on its surface. The new ball had only 14 panels, which resembled propeller blades or turbines.

According to the folks at Adidas, the new design resulted in a rounder ball with fewer seams. The more rounded shape meant that the ball would respond more predictably to the force of a kick. Fewer seams meant that the ball would experience less turbulence as it flew through the air. To help reduce drag even further, the +Teamgeist ball had seams that were glued together rather than stitched together. Also, instead of being made from flat panels that are then bent into shape, the "propellers" of the new ball were premolded to be curved.

Before Adidas released the ball, they did extensive lab testing. This included having a robotic leg kick the ball into a wall several thousand times. The ball behaved as it was meant to. The kicks appeared to be much straighter, and the rebounds much truer. Adidas engineers then took the ball to Loughborough University in the United Kingdom, where it was tested further. Everything seemed fine, until the ball was used in games. Complaints started coming in from goalkeepers who were trying to catch it.

It turned out that the +Teamgeist was much more unpredictable than anyone imagined. Part of the problem was that the ball was so aerodynamic that once it started moving through the air, it had a very low spin rate. As you may recall, a spinning ball will follow a fairly straight line unless the spin is off to one side, in which case it will curve. Instead of spinning, the +Teamgeist would just sort of flutter through the air, like a knuckleball thrown by a baseball pitcher.

In the end, despite the goalkeepers' unhappiness, the

Scientists created the +Teamgeist soccer ball—which, unlike a traditional soccer ball, has turbine-shaped panels and glued seams—to provide less turbulence and drag, as well as to respond more predictably to the force of a kick. Though it actually behaved more unpredictably than was originally planned, it is still used today. Here, France's Zinedine Zidane shoots a +Teamgeist ball before the World Cup final match against Italy in 2006.

introduction of the new ball was not a disaster. Because it resulted in higher-scoring soccer games, most soccer fans seemed happy. Since the +Teamgeist was introduced in 2006, goalies have learned to adapt somewhat to its chaotic movements, though most would probably prefer to play with the traditional ball. Maybe this is one case in which science should have stayed out of sports.

RUNNING SHOES GO GREEN

Have you ever wondered what happens to the millions of basketball sneakers, running shoes, and cross trainers that athletes (and the rest of us) wear out every year? Like most other unwanted things, they usually end up in the trash, often in landfills. Once shoes are buried in a landfill, it can take 1,000 years or more before they break down. This means there are a lot of landfills filling up with a lot of sneakers.

In an effort to save some landfill space, scientists working at Brooks Running have come up with a new kind of foam that biodegrades 50 times faster than a standard running shoe. The company says this will save more than 30 million pounds of waste in landfills over the next 20 years. The secret is an additive called BioMoGo. This nontoxic substance encourages anaerobic microbes that live in landfills to eat the shoe. Yet, people don't have to worry about their shoes being eaten when they put them away in their closets. As you may recall, *anaerobic* means without oxygen. As long as the shoes are above ground where there is plenty of air, they should be fine!

FIELDING THE FUTURE

Many people think that science and sports are two separate subjects. After reading this text, however, you can see how they actually work quite nicely together. It's hard to tell just what the future will bring for either discipline, but both science and sports will continue to change over time. If anything, science is going to play even a bigger role in sports in the future.

In all likelihood, advances in science may mean that some of the games as we know them will change and new games will develop. Thirty years ago, very few people were snowboarding, and the X Games didn't exist. New advances in science will mean that athletic equipment will continue to improve. Coupled with the fact that science is helping to produce stronger and faster athletes, all of this means that old sports records will continue to be broken. While this may upset some people, others look at it as part of the game.

As a wise man once said, you have to be in it to win it. So don't just sit there: Go out and play with some science!

Glossary

Acceleration   The change in speed or direction of a moving object

Aerobic   A chemical reaction that needs oxygen in order to take place

Anaerobic   A chemical reaction that takes place without oxygen

Angular momentum   A property of an object moving around some fixed point. Angular momentum depends on an object's mass, velocity, and radius.

ATP (adenosine triphosphate)   A molecule that provides fuel to the body's cells

Center of gravity   Also called the "center of mass," it is the point in an object at which all the mass appears to be concentrated

Coefficient of restitution   The degree to which an object will rebound or bounce back

Energy   The ability to do work or make something move

Equilibrium   A state in which all the forces acting on an object balance one another. The object is either at rest or in motion at a constant speed and in a constant direction.

Feedback   A process where information is gathered and used to make an adjustment

Fitness   Being mentally and physically prepared to do an activity

Force   A push or pull, such as gravity or magnetism

Friction   A force of resistance between two objects when either or both are in motion

Gravity   A force of attraction between objects

Homeostasis   Maintaining an internal balance or steady state

Impulse   The product of a force and the duration of time that the force acts on an object

Inertia   The tendency of an object to maintain its current state of motion. Objects with greater mass have more inertia.

Lever   A simple machine that transfers energy and multiplies force

Momentum   The product of the mass of a moving object and its velocity or speed

Muscle endurance   A measure of how long or how often a set of muscles can be used before the muscles get tired and need to rest

Projectile   An object that is launched by some means and continues in motion due to its own inertia

Reaction time   A measure of how long it takes for a living thing to react to some type of change or stimulus

Resonance   An increase in the motion of an object brought about by a series of repetitive forces acting on that object

Rotational inertia   Inertia of an object that is moving around a fixed point, such as a bicycle wheel

Stress   The way the body reacts to different challenges or tasks

Testosterone   A hormone produced in both males and females, but in much higher levels in males

Vestibular system   The body system that controls the body's sense of balance

Bibliography

Dittman, Richard and Glenn Schmeig. *Physics In Everyday Life*. New York: McGraw Hill, 1979.

Hall, Joanna. *The Exercise Bible*. Guilford, Conn.: The Lyons Press, 2003.

Hewitt, Paul. *Touch This! Conceptual Physics for Everyone*. New York: Addison Wesley, 2002.

Merki, Mary and Don Merki. *Glencoe Health, A Guide to Wellness*, 4th edition. New York: Macmillan/McGraw Hill, 1994.

Villee, Claude, [et al.] *Biology. 2nd edition*. Philadelphia: Saunders College Publishing, 1989.

Further Resources

Basedow, John. *Fitness Made Simple.* New York: McGraw Hill, 2008.

Gardner, Robert. *Science Projects About the Physics of Sports.* Berkeley Heights, N.J.: Enslow Publishers, 2000.

Goodstein, Madeline. *Sports Science Projects.* Berkeley Heights, N.J.: Enslow Publishers, 1999.

Hall, Joanna. *The Exercise Bible.* Guilford, Conn.: The Lyons Press, 2003.

Hewitt, Paul. *Touch This! Conceptual Physics for Everyone.* New York: Addison Wesley, 2002.

Wood, Robert. *Mechanics Fundamentals.* Philadelphia: Chelsea House Publishers, 1999.

Web sites

Exploratorium: Sport Science
http://www.exploratorium.edu/sports/index.html
This Web site, produced by the Exploratorium Science Center in San Francisco, has a wealth of information dealing with the science behind many of the most popular sports. The site includes informative videos, articles, links to science try-its, and frequently asked questions dealing with the science of sports.

Planet SciCast
http://www.planet-scicast.com/
This Web site contains a collection of short movies covering a range of science topics, including many on the science of sports. Some of the movies feature demonstrations and have links to hands-on experiments.

Sport Videos
http://www.5min.com/Category/Sports
As the name suggests, this Web site contains dozens of short (5 minute) videos covering a wide range of sports science topics.

World of Sports Science

http://www.faqs.org/sports-science/index.html

This Web site contains literally hundreds of brief, scientifically accurate articles that connect science and sports. Topics include Strength Training and Sports, Motorcycle Racing, The Dynamics of Basketball Shots, and many more. The link above goes directly to the index of articles.

Picture Credits

Index

A

acceleration, 49. *See also* Controlling How Fast Objects Can Fall

adenosine triphosphate (ATP)
glucose and, 34
Type I/Type II muscles and, 41–42

Adidas, 145–146

aerobic process of oxidation, 36

air bags, 135

air resistance. *See* "drag"

anaerobic process
"green" technology and, 146
lactic acid and, 41–42
of oxidation, 36

angle of object. *See* How the Angle at which an Object is Thrown Affects Distance

angular momentum, 77. *See also* How Spinning Wheel Speed Affects Balance; Testing the Speed of Rotation
balance and, 78, 80
body's radius and, 82
radius of spinning object and, 81

Apollo 15 astronaut's experiment, 53–54

Applying Newton's Laws of Motion, 96–99
analysis, 98
our findings, 99
procedure, 97–98
time required/materials, 96
topic/introduction, 96
what's going on, 98–99

Armstrong, Lance, 55

athletic training techniques, 141

ATP. *See* adenosine triphosphate

B

balance. *See also* How Spinning Wheel Speed Affects Balance; Staying in Balance; Testing Your Center of Gravity
angular momentum and, 77
counterbalancing and, 75
equilibrium and, 72

balance beams, 85

"banana ball," 89

baseball. *See also* Hitting a Ball on Baseball Bat's "Sweet Spot"; Testing the Spin of a Spherical Ball
curveballs, 89
leverage and, 115
"setting up" to receive a throw, 134

basketball
"hang time" and, 45, 48
momentum and, 124
shoe design and, 64

bats. *See also* Hitting a Ball on Baseball Bat's "Sweet Spot"
"choking up" on, 115
"node" on, 109
"sweet spot" on, 106

Beckham, David, 89

bicycling, 144

blood supply. *See* Feeling Your Pulse

body builders, repetitions and, 38

body flexibility. *See* Measuring Body Flexibility

bouncing ball, 100. *See also* sports balls; Testing a Ball's Ability to Bounce

Brain Injury Association of America, 142

Brooks Running, 146

bungee cords, 135

C

center of gravity. *See also* Testing the Speed of Rotation; Testing Your Center of Gravity
balance and, 88
equilibrium and, 72

Changing the Impulse of a Force on a Soccer Ball, 127–130
analysis, 129
data table, 129
our findings, 130
procedure, 128
time required/materials, 127
topic/introduction, 127
what's going on, 129–130

circulation of blood. *See* Feeling Your Pulse

coefficient of restitution, 100

colliding objects. *See* Force of Colliding Objects, The

conditioning, 28

Controlling How Fast Objects Can Fall, 50–54
analysis, 53
data tables, 52–53

our findings, 54
procedure, 51–52
topic/introduction, 50
what's going on, 53–54
counterbalancing, 75
curveball, 89

D

"dead air zone," 55
divers. *See also* Testing the
    Speed of Rotation
    force of impact and, 131
    resonance and, 116
    rotational inertia and, 81
drafting, 55
"drag"
    speed of falling objects
        and, 54
    stitches, laces, dimples and,
        94
    wind, water and, 142–144
    wind-tunnel tests for, 144

E

ear, structures of the, 20–21
energy transfer. *See* Laws of
    Motion
equilibrium
    center of gravity and, 72
    vestibular system and,
        19–21

F

falling bodies, 49. *See also*
    Controlling How Fast
    Objects Can Fall
"fast twitch" muscle fibers, 41,
    42, 43
fatigue
    ATP and, 36
    men's muscles and, 43
    reaction time and, 27
feedback systems. *See also*
    Staying in Balance
    reaction time and, 26
    at work and play, 17

Feeling Your Pulse, 13–16
    analysis, 15
    data table, 15
    our findings, 16
    procedure, 14
    time required/materials,
        13
    topic/introduction, 13
    what's going on, 15–16
females, gender gap and, 43
figure skaters, 81. *See also*
    Testing the Speed of
    Rotation
fitness, 12
flexibility. *See* Measuring Body
    Flexibility
"follow through" of ball,
    129–130
football. *See also* Throwing a
    Football
    air resistance, footballs
        and, 54
    helmets for, 136, 139, 140,
        142
    inertia and, 76
    projectile motion and, 55
    putting spin on ball, 89
    rotational inertia and, 85
    shape of ball and, 88
football helmets, brief history
    of, 140
footwear, 146. *See also* How
    Shoe Design Affects Friction
force
    air resistance, 54, 55
    equilibrium and, 72
    friction, 60, 67
    of gravity, 26, 44, 50, 59
    impulse and, 127, 129–130,
        131
Force of Colliding Objects, The,
    132–134
    analysis, 134
    our findings, 134
    procedure, 133
    time required/materials,
        132
    topic/introduction, 132
    what's going on, 134

friction. *See also* "drag"; How
    Lubricant Affects Friction;
    How Shoe Design Affects
    Friction
    air resistance and, 60
    gravity and, 67
fulcrum, lever and, 111, 112,
    114–115
future of sports, 141–147
    building a better bike, 144
    fielding the future, 146–147
    NASA swimsuits, 142–144
    running shoes go green,
        146
    soccer ball shape, 144–146

G

Galileo Galilei
    acceleration and, 49
    death of, 95
    gravity and, 59
    speed of falling objects, 50,
        53–54
gender gap, 43
glucose, muscle cells and, 34, 36
golf balls, 94
gravity, force of. *See also* How
    Gravity Affects Jumping;
    Testing Your Center of
    Gravity
    air resistance and, 54
    angle at which an object is
        thrown, 59
    center of gravity, 72
    described, 44
    falling bodies and, 49
    friction and, 67
    reaction time and, 26
    speed of falling objects, 50
"green" technology, 146
gymnasts
    balance beams and, 85
    speed of rotation and, 82

H

"hang time," 45, 48, 56
hardball, playing, 106

Head Impact Telemetry System (HITS), 142
head injuries, 142
heart rate, 16
helmets. *See also* Testing Safety Helmet Materials
    football helmets, history, 140
    high-tech helmets, 142
    padding for, 136
high divers, 81. *See also* Testing the Speed of Rotation
high-tech helmets, 142
Hitting a Ball on Baseball Bat's "Sweet Spot," 107–110
    analysis, 109
    our findings, 110
    procedure, 108–109
    time required/materials, 107
    topic/introduction, 107
    what's going on, 109–110
hockey masks, 136
homeostasis, 12
How a Leg Acts Like a Lever, 112–115
    analysis, 114
    our findings, 115
    procedure, 113–114
    time required/materials, 112–113
    topic/introduction, 112
    what's going on, 114–115
How Gravity Affects Jumping, 45–48
    analysis, 48
    data table, 47
    our findings, 48
    procedure, 46–47
    time required/materials, 45
    topic/introduction, 45
    what's going on, 48
How Lubricant Affects Friction, 67–71
    data tables, 69–70
    our findings, 71
    procedure, 68–69
    time required/materials, 67–68

topic/introduction, 67
    what's going on, 71
How Mass and Velocity Affect Momentum of a Moving Object, 122–125
    analysis, 124
    our findings, 124–125
    procedure, 123
    time required/materials, 122
    topic/introduction, 122
    what's going on, 124
How Resonance Affects Motion, 117–119
    analysis, 119
    our findings, 119
    procedure, 118–119
    time required/materials, 117
    topic/introduction, 117
    what's going on, 119
How Shoe Design Affects Friction, 61–65
    analysis, 64
    data tables, 63–64
    our findings, 65
    procedure, 62–63
    time required/materials, 62
How Spinning Wheel Speed Affects Balance, 78–80
    analysis, 80
    our findings, 80
    procedure, 79–80
    time required/materials, 78
    topic/introduction, 78
    what's going on, 80
How the Angle at which an Object is Thrown Affects Distance, 56–59
    analysis, 58–59
    data table, 58
    our findings, 59
    procedure, 57–58
    time required/materials, 57
    topic/introduction, 56
    what's going on, 59
human vestibular system, 19–21

I
impulse, 131. *See also* Changing the Impulse of a Force on a Soccer Ball; Force of Colliding Objects, The
inertia
    defined, 88
    Law of Inertia, 96
    mass and, 121
    projectile motion and, 55
    rotational inertia, 77, 81, 85
    understanding concept of, 76

J
Jankovic, Jelena, 28
joints, flexibility and, 31–32
jumping. *See* How Gravity Affects Jumping

L
labyrinth, inner ear and, 20–21
lactate, 36–37
lactic acid
    building in muscle cells, 42
    fermentation of, 36–37
Laws of Motion. *See also* Applying Newton's Laws of Motion
    energy transfer and, 95, 120
    First Law of Motion, 76, 121
    Law of Acceleration, 96
    Law of Action/Reaction, 96, 100, 120
    Law of Inertia, 96, 120
leverage, 111. *See also* How a Leg Acts Like a Lever
lifting weights. *See* weight training
ligaments, 32
lubricants, 66. *See also* How Lubricant Affects Friction

M
Magnus, Heinrich, 92
Magnus effect, 93

males, testosterone and, 43
marathon runners, 16
mass. *See also* How Mass and
    Velocity Affect Momentum
    of a Moving Object
    air resistance and, 54
    angular momentum and,
        84
    center of gravity and,
        82
    inertia and, 76, 121
Measuring Body Flexibility,
    29–32
    analysis, 31
    data table, 31
    our findings, 32
    procedure, 30–31
    time required/materials,
        29
    topic/introduction, 29
    what's going on, 31–32
Measuring Human Reaction
    Time, 23–27
    analysis, 25
    data table, 25
    our findings, 27
    procedure, 23–24
    time required/materials,
        23
    topic/introduction, 23
    what's going on, 26–27
momentum. *See also* How
    Mass and Velocity Affect
    Momentum of a Moving
    Object
    angular momentum, 78,
        80
    changing of, 126
    collision and, 134
    moving objects and, 77
    speed and, 135
    water and, 131
motion. *See* Laws of Motion
muscles. *See also* Pushing
    Muscles to the Limit
    glucose and, 34, 36
    making of, 33
    "muscle spindles," 32
    skeletal muscle, 38

N
National Football League,
    140
Newton, Sir Isaac
    First Law of Motion, 76,
        121
    Laws of Motion, 95–99,
        120
    spinning ball and, 92

O
oxidation of glucose, 34, 36, 37

P
padding with a purpose, 136.
    See also Testing Safety
    Helmet Materials
Phelps, Michael, 143
physical conditioning, 28
physical fitness, sports and,
    12
projectile motion, 55
protective gear, 136. *See also*
    Testing Safety Helmet
    Materials
pulse. *See* Feeling Your Pulse
Pushing Muscles to the Limit,
    34–37
    analysis, 36
    data table, 36
    our findings, 37
    procedure, 35
    time required/materials,
        34
    topic/introduction, 34
    what's going on, 36–37

Q
quickness vs. speed, 22. *See also*
    Measuring Human Reaction
    Time

R
range of motion, 31

reaction time. *See also*
    Measuring Human Reaction
    Time
    described, 22
    fatigue and, 27
rebound. *See* Testing a Ball's
    Ability to Bounce
recovery time, heart rate and,
    16
resonance, 116. *See also* How
    Resonance Affects Motion
Revolution football helmet,
    142
Riddell Company, 140, 142
Rockne, Knute, 140
rotational inertia. *See also*
    How Spinning Wheel Speed
    Affects Balance; Testing the
    Speed of Rotation; Throwing
    a Football
    balance beams and, 85
    momentum and, 77
    subtle moves and, 81
Rozenberg, Pavlo, 116
runners
    marathon runners, 16
    weight training for, 38
Running Distances vs. Speed,
    39–42
    analysis, 41
    data table, 41
    our findings, 42
    procedure, 40
    time required/materials,
        39
    topic/introduction, 39
    what's going on, 41–42

S
safety. *See* Testing Safety
    Helmet Materials
safety precautions, experiments
    and, 8–10
    chemicals and, 9
    equipment use and, 9
    finishing up, 10
    general precautions, 8
    heating substances, 9–10

preparing for experiment, 8

protecting yourself, 9

reviewing experiment, 8

Santana, Johan, 89

Scott, David, 53

shape, air resistance and, 54

shoe design, 146. *See also* How Shoe Design Affects Friction

skateboarding, 116, 120. *See also* Applying Newton's Laws of Motion

skaters, 81. *See also* Testing the Speed of Rotation

skeletal muscle

two types of fibers in, 41

weight training and, 38

skiers, waxes for, 71

"slow twitch" muscle fibers, 41, 42

snowboarding, 146

soccer/soccer balls. *See also* Changing the Impulse of a Force on a Soccer Ball; Testing the Spin of a Spherical Ball

+Teamgeist soccer ball, 145–146

"banana ball," 89

leverage and, 114–115

soccer ball shape, 144–146

World Cup tournament, 145

softball, 124. *See also* Force of Colliding Objects, The

speed. *See* Controlling How Fast Objects Can Fall; Testing the Speed of Rotation

speed vs. quickness, 22. *See also* Measuring Human Reaction Time

Speedo LZR swimsuit, 143–144

Speedo's Aqualab development team, 144

spinning wheel. *See* How Spinning Wheel Speed Affects Balance

sports balls. *See also* specific sport

bouncing ball, 100

stitches, laces, and dimples of, 94

SuperBall, 106

sports equipment. *See* future of sports

Staying in Balance, 18–21

analysis, 19

our findings, 21

procedure, 19

structures of ear and, 20–21

time required/materials, 18

topic/introduction, 18

what's going on, 19–21

stresses, fitness and, 12

stretching

flexibility and, 32

stretch test, 31–32

SuperBall, 106

"sweet spot." *See* Hitting a Ball on Baseball Bat's "Sweet Spot"

swimsuits, NASA, 142–144

T

t'ai chi, 32

+Teamgeist soccer ball, 145

technology. *See* future of sports

tennis ball, 105

Testing a Ball's Ability to Bounce, 101–105

analysis, 104

data tables, 103–104

our findings, 105

procedure, 102–103

time required/materials, 101

topic/introduction, 101

what's going on, 105

Testing Safety Helmet Materials, 137–139

analysis, 139

our findings, 139

procedure, 138–139

time required/materials, 137

topic/introduction, 137

what's going on, 139

Testing the Speed of Rotation, 82–84

analysis, 84

our findings, 84

procedure, 82–83

time required/materials, 82

topic/introduction, 82

what's going on, 84

Testing the Spin of a Spherical Ball, 90–93

analysis, 92

our findings, 93

procedure, 91–92

time required/materials, 90

topic/introduction, 90

what's going on, 92–93

Testing Your Center of Gravity, 73–75

analysis, 75

our findings, 75

procedure, 73–74

time required/materials, 73

topic/introduction, 73

what's going on, 75

testosterone, 43

throwing. *See* How the Angle at which an Object is Thrown Affects; Testing the Spin of a Spherical Ball

Throwing a Football, 86–88

our findings, 88

procedure, 86–88

time required/materials, 86

topic/introduction, 86

what's going on, 88

trainers, 141
Type I/Type II muscle fibers, 41, 43

V

velocity. *See* How Mass and Velocity Affect Momentum of a Moving Object
vestibular system, 19–21

W

wax/oil, 66. *See also* How Lubricant Affects Friction
weight training, 38
wheel speed. *See* How Spinning Wheel Speed Affects Balance
Wilkinson, Steve, 143–144

X

X Games, 146

Y

yoga, 32

About the Author

STEPHEN M. TOMECEK is a scientist and big-time sports fan who enjoys hiking, biking, and playing basketball. He is the author of more than 30 nonfiction books for both children and teachers, including *Bouncing & Bending Light,* the 1996 winner of the American Institute of Physics Science Writing Award. Steve also works as a consultant and writer for The National Geographic Society and Scholastic Inc.